Financing Firm Growth

Scan the QR code to see all titles in this series.

International Finance Corporation Research Series

The International Finance Corporation (IFC) Research Series explores the mobilization of private sector capital in support of development and the elimination of poverty in a livable world. Publications are subject to review meetings chaired by the IFC managing director and the vice president of economics. Relevant regional or industry vice presidents and directors also participate. The peer reviewers include experts from outside the World Bank Group.

Books in the series

Financing Firm Growth: The Role of Capital Markets in Low- and Middle-Income Countries, Cesaire A. Meh and Sergio L. Schmukler, editors, 2025

Digital Opportunities in African Businesses, Marcio Cruz, editor, 2024

All books in the International Finance Corporation
Research Series are available for free at
https://hdl.handle.net/10986/41286.

INTERNATIONAL FINANCE CORPORATION RESEARCH SERIES

Financing Firm Growth

The Role of Capital Markets in Low- and Middle-Income Countries

Edited by Cesaire A. Meh and Sergio L. Schmukler

WORLD BANK GROUP

CONTENTS

Chapter 4. Economic Outcomes of Issuing Capital   47
Manuel García-Santana

Chapter 5. Drivers of Capital Market Growth
and Policy Implications   67
Alvaro Pedraza and Imtiaz Ul Haq

Boxes

Figures

Map

Tables

FOREWORD

Capital markets can have a transformative impact on firms and economies. They are an increasingly important source of firm financing, particularly for innovative, long-term, and capital-intensive projects. By enabling efficient allocation of funds toward productive firms, capital markets foster private sector growth, which, in turn, boosts employment and productivity across the broader economy. Yet capital markets in low- and middle-income countries still lag behind those in advanced economies. This persists even as financing needs by firms in these markets intensify, driven by rapid technological advancements, tighter financing conditions, and the reshaping of global supply chains.

This research presents new data and analysis on how firms in emerging and developing economies have accessed debt and equity capital markets over the past 30 years. It provides granular evidence on which firms participate as capital markets grow, the implications for firm growth, and the broader economic effects on productivity. By examining over 20,000 firms across 106 low- and middle-income countries and economies, this book offers novel insights on capital market financing for firms. It also presents measures to promote such financing. We find encouraging evidence that there has been progress in recent decades, with more and smaller firms from a growing number of low- and middle-income countries tapping into capital markets. However, more needs to be done to address the remaining gaps.

Capital markets are important to private sector growth and are therefore central to our work. The World Bank Group/IFC has long been a leader in promoting capital market development in emerging markets by being an anchor investor in new issuances, and through research, capacity-building, and strategic injections of capital. Over decades of work, including pioneering new types of data collection on emerging stock markets and supporting local-currency transactions, we have helped to advance these markets.

I am confident that the insights presented in this book will further efforts to support investors. Such information is critical for investors for whom emerging markets may otherwise appear opaque and risky. The accompanying Capital Markets portal is a step toward enhancing transparency on key firm characteristics. I hope all stakeholders—both public and private—interested in capital markets in low- and middle-income countries will find this book and the portal to be invaluable resources for deepening their understanding and shaping the future of these markets.

Makhtar Diop
Managing Director
International Finance Corporation

ACKNOWLEDGMENTS

This book was prepared under the guidance of Susan Lund, Vice President for Economics and Private Sector Development, International Finance Corporation (IFC), and Paolo Mauro, Director of IFC's Economics and Market Research Department. In addition, Indermit Gill, Senior Vice President for Development Economics (DEC) and World Bank Group Chief Economist; Roumeen Islam, Senior Economic Adviser to the IFC Managing Director; and Denis Medvedev, Senior Economic Adviser, provided support and guidance.

The book was written jointly by an IFC and DEC team, led by Cesaire A. Meh, Manager, and Sergio L. Schmukler, Research Manager, with significant contributions from Imtiaz Ul Haq. The core team comprised Manuel García-Santana, Pablo Hernando-Kaminsky, Alvaro Pedraza, and Imtiaz Ul Haq. Matias Moretti contributed to an early draft of the book.

Furthermore, Brian Castro Aguirre, Juliana Beall, Dmitri Kirpichev Cherezov, Miquel Lorente, Paolo Sabella, and Matias Gonzalo Soria provided excellent support on data used in the analysis. We are also grateful to Nicolas Cogorno for developing the accompanying online Capital Markets Portal.

The team benefited from numerous interactions with researchers from academia and international policy institutions. Natalie Bau from the University of California at Los Angeles (UCLA), Stijn Claessens from Yale University, Julian Di Giovanni from the Federal Reserve Bank of New York, Deniz Igan from the Bank for International Settlements, and Augusto de la Torre from Columbia University peer reviewed the book.

Peer reviewers from IFC included Alfonso Garcia Mora, with additional comments from Jeff Anderson, John Gandolfo, Mohamed Gouled, Roumeen Islam, Morgan Landy, and Tomasz Telma. Dilek Aykut, Marcio Cruz, Kianna Freeman, Jacqueline T. Irving, Maty Konte, Ralf Martin, Florian Moelders, Mariana Pereira-Lopez, Zeinab Partow, Rey Zhangrui Wang, Verena Wiedemann, and Nadege Yameogo contributed with additional discussions.

Peer reviewers from the World Bank included Ana Paula Cusolito, Erik Feyen, and Jean Pesme, with additional comments from Deon Filmer, Indermit Gill, and Norman Loayza. Juan Jose Cortina, Robert Cull, Tatiana Didier, and Ana Fiorella Carvajal provided valuable feedback.

The book also benefited from discussions with participants in the IFC and Jeune Afrique's third annual Africa Financial Industry Summit, hosted in Morocco, as well as during presentations at Columbia University, the 27th Congreso de Tesorería, Asobancaria, Colombia, the International Christian University in Tokyo, and the Southern Economic Association.

We thank Erik Churchill, David Harrison, and Chris Vellacott from IFC's publications team for their editorial contributions, as well as Irina Sarchenko for significant help with graphic design. Bruce Ross-Larson led the editorial process of the earlier version of the book. We are also grateful to the World Bank Group's editorial production team, including Jewel McFadden, acquisitions editor; Mary Fisk, production editor; and Melina Rose Yingling, designer, for the marketing, production, and design of this book, and to the IFC communications team, including Erik Churchill and Monica De Leon, for their creative energy in promoting the book. We also thank Adama Badji, Gleice De Marrocos, Sabrina Islam, Linette Malago, Irina Tolstaia, Carmen Andira Watson, and Fatima Yousofi for their exceptional administrative support.

This book is a product of IFC's Economics and Private Sector Development Vice Presidency and DEC. The team wishes to express its appreciation to the Joint Capital Markets Program (J-CAP), and in this case to the Ministry of Finance of Luxembourg, which financially supported this study under J-CAP.

EXECUTIVE SUMMARY

Capital Markets Have Been Financing Firms Around the Globe

Over the past three decades, capital market financing has surged for firms in low- and middle-income countries.[1] This growth is not confined to a few established corporates but includes a broad spectrum of firms from an increasing number of countries. Firms are deploying this capital to become more productive—investing in physical assets, hiring more workers, and expanding operations, spurring growth both at the firm level and within their economies.

This book analyzes data from nearly 80,000 firms worldwide, focusing on how the 20,000 firms located in 106 low- and middle-income countries access and use capital market financing. Leveraging a novel database of global bond and equity issuances between 1990 and 2022, the findings reveal that the expansion of capital market financing has facilitated access for smaller, younger, and more productive firms than those already participating (box ES.1 introduces a tool for analyzing the data). These firms have subsequently experienced significant growth in physical capital, employment, and sales. The book explores potential drivers behind the capital market expansion, focusing on the role of economic growth and supportive policies.

BOX ES.1

Using the Capital Markets Portal

While focusing on low- and middle-income countries, the book analyzes many patterns of capital market financing of firms for all countries in the world. For readers interested in alternative comparisons, the companion Capital Markets Portal, https://capitalmarketsportal.worldbank.org, is an online tool that allows users to reproduce figures and tables from the book for any country and region of their choice and to compare them across desired benchmarks.

Debt and Equity Issuances Have Surged in Low- and Middle-Income Countries

To measure the expansion of capital markets, this book focuses on cumulative net capital issuance (CNI)—the sum of equity issuances and bond issuances since the beginning of the period minus bonds that have matured. The book examines the 1990–2022 period to uncover long-run trends in capital market activity. The analysis focuses only on firms participating in capital markets. Although these firms are a small fraction of the total number of firms, they typically account for a large share of national income as they tend to be large firms.

Firms from low- and middle-income countries raised CNI of US$4 trillion from bond and equity markets between 1990 and 2022, much of it coming after the turn of the millennium (figure ES.1).[2] From 2000 to 2022, CNI increased fourfold in middle-income countries and eightfold in low-income countries. The CNI in these two groups of countries doubled as a share of gross domestic product (GDP) in the same period.

FIGURE ES.1

Firms Significantly Expanded Their Capital Market Financing in Low- and Middle-Income Countries

US$, billions

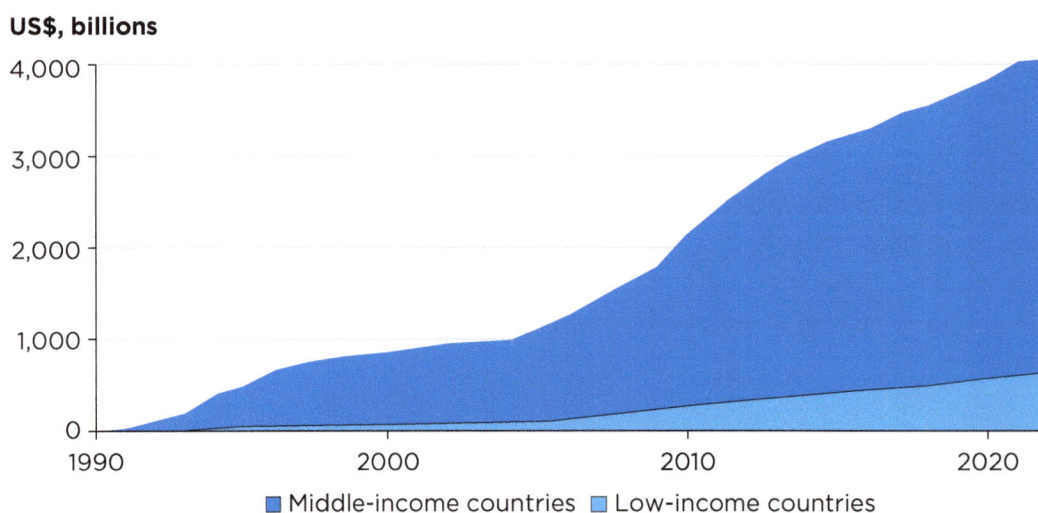

Source: Calculations using issuance data from the Securities Data Company Platinum database from LSEG.
Note: This figure shows the CNI of nonfinancial firms for the 1990–2022 period in billions of 2020 dollars for low- and middle-income countries. CNI each year is calculated as the sum of equity issuances and bond issuances since 1990, minus bonds that have matured since 1990 for each country group. Appendix B provides the list of countries, grouped by income category, following the World Bank classification for the year 1990. CNI = cumulative net capital issuance.

Capital market financing in low- and middle-income countries has grown faster than bank financing since the early 1990s. Although banks remain the primary providers of external finance for most firms, capital markets are becoming an important alternative for a growing number of companies. Even firms that rely on banks or other sources for their financing can benefit from the rise in capital markets. Capital market growth can unlock financing for small firms by freeing up bank credit or enhancing access through linkages with issuing companies. Capital markets also facilitate private equity investments by providing exit opportunities via initial public offerings.

The expansion of capital markets attracted a significant influx of new firms, which captured a large share of the funds raised in these markets (figure ES.2). From 2000 to their peak in 2021, the number of nonfinancial firms issuing bonds or equities annually increased 300 percent in low- and middle-income countries versus 40 percent in high-income countries. Around 14,000 firms became new participants in capital markets in low- and middle-income countries between 2000 and 2022. Moreover, firms from 32 middle-income countries and 13 low-income countries accessed capital markets for the first time during this period.

FIGURE ES.2

The Expansion of Capital Market Financing Was Associated with a Growing Number of New Issuers in Low- and Middle-Income Countries

Number of new issuers each year

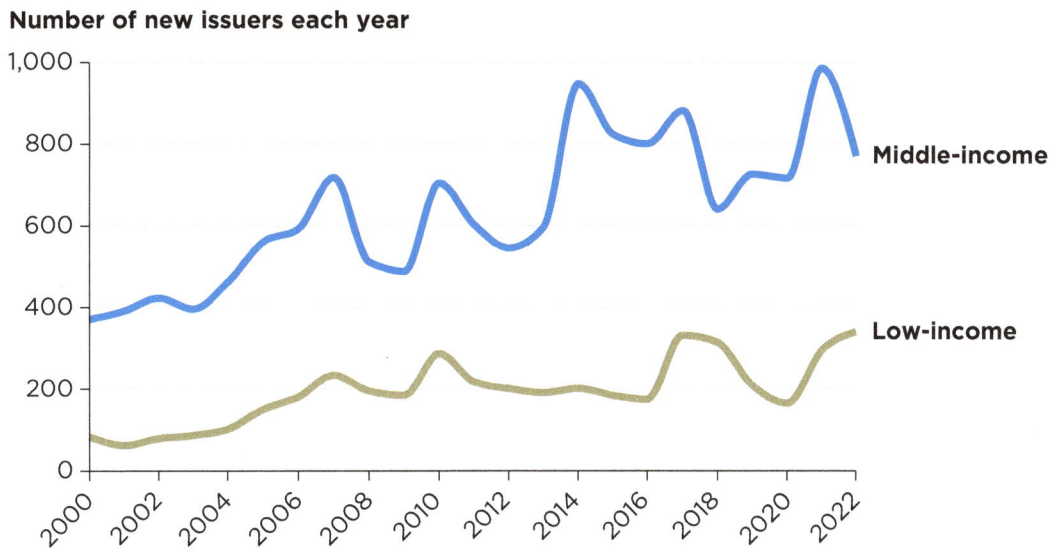

Source: Calculations using issuance data from the Securities Data Company Platinum database from LSEG.
Note: This figure shows the number of firms entering capital markets from 2000 to 2022 for low- and middle-income countries. Each year, only firms that issued for the first time are counted. Appendix B provides the list of countries, grouped by income category, following the World Bank classification for the year 1990.

Domestic bond and equity markets, primarily in local currencies, have been the driving force behind this growth in low- and middle-income countries. Between 1990 and 2022, domestic markets accounted for more than half of total issuance (53 percent for bonds and 79 percent for equities). Moreover, the average size of individual domestic bond issuances decreased by approximately 30 percent between 2000–09 and 2010–22 for firms raising funds in capital markets for the first time. Since small firms typically issue smaller amounts, the decline in average size of domestic bond issuances suggests that access to domestic capital markets has become easier for them. In contrast, the size of bond issuances in international markets increased during the same period, indicating that larger firms were tapping into international capital markets.

As capital markets expanded, a broader range of firms gained access to financing, with a greater share of funds allocated to smaller, younger, more productive, and financially more constrained firms than those already participating in capital markets. New participants—firms that accessed capital markets only from 2000 onward—accounted for more than 60 percent of CNI in low- and middle-income countries by 2022. By contrast, new participants accounted for 42 percent of CNI in high-income countries. Compared to firms that accessed capital markets in the 1990s, these new participants were younger and smaller in relation to sales, physical capital, and employment.

At the time of issuance, new participants in low- and middle-income countries had higher marginal returns to capital (defined as the additional output a company generates from using an extra unit of capital) than firms in the same industry and country that were active in capital markets in the 1990s. For this reason, investing in these firms had the potential to yield a greater increase in production or profits, making them particularly effective recipients of new capital.

How Capital Markets Can Boost Investment, Employment, and Output

The impact of capital market participation on firms and the broader economy hinges on whether firms use the funds raised for productive activities. This book presents new evidence that firms used the proceeds to invest in productive assets. In the first year after raising capital, these firms' investment in physical capital rose 16 percent in low-income countries and 8 percent in middle-income countries, with some of these effects persisting for years (figure ES.3). This increase in physical capital was associated with an increase in both employment and sales.

FIGURE ES.3

Firms in Low- and Middle-Income Countries Exhibited Strong
Growth in Physical Capital after Capital Market Issuance

Cumulative change from year before issuance (%)

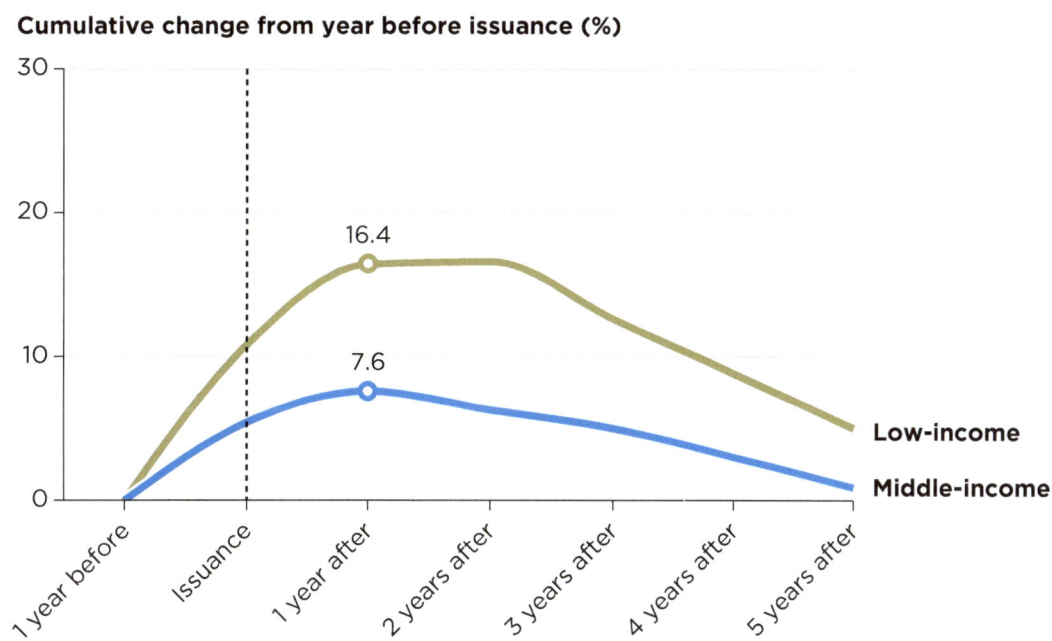

Sources: Calculations using issuance data from the Securities Data Company Platinum
database and firms balance sheet data from Worldscope, both from LSEG.
Note: This figure shows the estimated cumulative impact of a firm's issuing activity on its
physical capital in low-income countries and middle-income countries. The baseline for
estimating cumulative impact is the year before issuance. Appendix B provides the list of
countries, grouped by income category.

**The effects of capital market issuances on firm growth vary depending on the
issuer and the financial instruments used.** The impact on growth is particularly
strong for new participants, despite their smaller issuances, as it appears to
alleviate their financial constraints. The estimates suggest that first-time issuances
offer greater relief from financial constraints than subsequent ones. The positive
effects on firm growth are twice as strong for equity issuances as for all bond
issuances (including refinancing)—perhaps reflecting the greater flexibility that
equity financing provides without the pressure of regular, fixed debt payments.
For instance, equity issuances are associated with a 13 percent increase in
physical capital, compared with a 5 percent increase in bond issuances. These
results are consistent with the idea that firms with high growth potential may
prefer to issue equity over bonds.

At the economywide level, the findings suggest that capital is being allocated more efficiently. Firms' participation in capital markets is linked to increases in a country's total stock of physical capital—measured as firms' property, plant, and equipment—and employment levels. In low-income countries, firm issuance activity accounted for 21 percent of the growth in physical capital and 12 percent of the growth in employment among publicly listed firms between 2000 and 2022. In middle-income countries, these estimates are 22 percent and 20 percent, respectively. Because firms with higher marginal returns to capital raised more funds, capital markets allocated capital more efficiently across firms, resulting in a greater impact on output. New participants in capital markets in the 2000s were especially important drivers of these positive effects.

Economic Growth and Policy Reforms Can Drive Capital Market Expansion

The expansion of capital market financing in low- and middle-income countries is related to domestic economic growth. Economic growth increases the supply of capital by increasing investable savings for households and boosts demand by expanding business opportunities for firms. The book finds that GDP growth is significantly associated with capital market expansion, accounting for nearly half of the variation in CNI across countries.

Policies to increase investable savings, such as moving to a prefunded pension system, can also spur fundraising in capital markets. Moving to a prefunded pension system is associated with stronger growth of domestic capital markets. Mandating retirement contributions by workers in individually funded accounts promotes the growth of private investment and pension funds, giving firms access to a new pool of savings. In low- and middle-income countries that undertook such reforms between 1990 and 2022, domestic CNI (as a share of GDP) increased close to five times in the four years following reform, whereas international issuance did not rise significantly (figure ES.4).

Reforms liberalizing international financial flows can allow firms to access a broader range of funding sources. For example, Colombia experienced several rounds of financial liberalization over the past three decades, with reforms including easing capital restrictions, simplifying access to investment products by foreign investors, enhancing access to foreign financial services, and offering preferential tax incentives for foreign investors. Low- and middle-income countries undertaking such liberalization reforms experienced a boost in international bond issuances, but not in domestic ones.

FIGURE ES.4

Countries with Pension Reforms Experienced Higher CNI in Domestic Markets

Change in CNI (% of GDP)

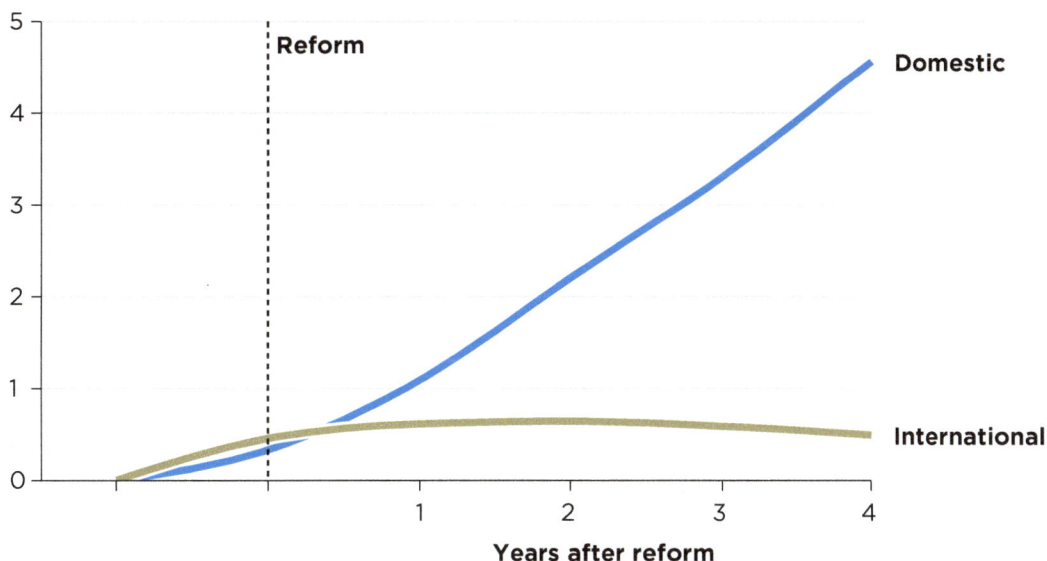

Years after reform

Sources: Calculations using data from the Securities Data Company Platinum database from LSEG and the International Federation of Pension Fund Administrators and GDP data from the World Bank's World Development Indicators.

Note: The sample includes 30 low- and middle-income countries with pension reforms introducing mandatory or quasi-mandatory individually funded programs between 1990 and 2022 (chapter 5 provides a list of these countries, and appendix O details the methodology used). The figure shows the impact of major pension reforms on domestic and foreign issuance activity beyond what would be expected in a counterfactual drawing on a control group of 117 countries from various income groups that did not implement major pension reforms during the sample period. The event year is defined as the year when the first major pension reform was implemented in each country. The vertical axis shows the total change in the CNI as a proportion of GDP, relative to the year before the reform. The ratio of CNI to GDP for year Y is computed as the sum of equity issuance, bond issuance (minus bonds that matured), or both between 1990 and year Y, divided by GDP in year Y. In the baseline year (that is, one year before reform) domestic and foreign CNI was 0.7 percent and 1.7 percent of domestic GDP, respectively. Point estimates are presented controlling for year and country fixed effects. CNI = cumulative net capital issuance; GDP = gross domestic product.

Policies focused on improving financial intermediation can also facilitate the transfer of funds from investors to firms. For instance, developing pricing benchmarks, such as a yield curve through sovereign issuances, can be critical for pricing corporate issuances as countries gain access to capital markets. For this reason, first-time sovereign issuances usually preceded initial corporate issuances in low- and middle-income countries. Strengthening investor protections and improving the domestic information environment can also reduce investors' expropriation risks and information costs. Stronger regulations on both these fronts are associated with higher domestic CNI (as a share of GDP).

Sustained capital market development requires comprehensive domestic reforms that encompass a broad set of policy measures, rather than isolated initiatives. Firms can supplement these measures by undertaking internal measures to reduce risks to investors, such as improving their corporate governance or voluntarily disclosing material information beyond mandated levels.

What Are the Key Takeaways?

Deeper domestic capital markets can scale up private investment in low- and middle-income countries and channel resources to the most productive firms. The book shows that domestic capital—to an even greater extent than foreign capital—has been a crucial source of private financing. Domestic markets can channel funds in local currencies to firms with high growth opportunities. More generally, developing domestic bond and equity markets can help local investors to fund the expansion of financially constrained firms, with beneficial effects for the economy overall.

Notes

1. Low- and middle-income countries are classified based on World Bank income classifications in 1990 (the beginning of the sample period). Appendix B presents the list of countries by income groups. Throughout the book, all references to low- and middle-income countries exclude China, which is treated separately given its economic ascent and size as well as its shift from low-income to middle-income status during the period under consideration.
2. All dollar amounts are inflation-adjusted 2020 US dollars unless otherwise indicated.

CHAPTER 1

Introduction

Cesaire A. Meh, Alvaro Pedraza, and Sergio L. Schmukler

Capital Markets Have a Growing Role in Economic Development

Well-functioning capital markets can foster economic growth and facilitate better resource allocation.[1] They are a fundamental source of financing for many firms, allowing them to tap into a broader base of funding, often at cheaper rates and with longer maturities than bank loans.[2] Over the past three decades, net issuance on capital markets has grown more rapidly than gross domestic product (GDP) across the world. For instance, the average cumulative net capital issuance (CNI), as a share of GDP, among financial and nonfinancial firms in 2016–22 was roughly nine times higher than in 1990–95 in low-income countries and seven times higher in middle-income countries (figure 1.1).[3] Capital markets in low- and middle-income countries have also expanded faster than bank financing since the early 1990s. Although banks remain the primary providers of external finance for most firms, capital markets are becoming an important alternative for an ever-expanding range of firms.[4]

This book explores the extent to which capital markets serve as a source of financing for firms globally, with a focus on low- and middle-income countries. A better understanding of the implications of the growth of capital markets requires further exploration to determine whether this expansion of capital markets activity reflects fundraising by a few established corporates or by a wider range of firms from more countries. To the extent that these markets allow firms to relax their financial constraints, new funds will lead to changes in their productive structure, which can then affect the overall economy. The book thus connects the financial and real economic activity of firms by systematically documenting new stylized facts around the world, paying special attention to firms in low- and middle-income countries.

FIGURE 1.1

Capital Market Financing Is Growing Faster Than Bank Financing Worldwide

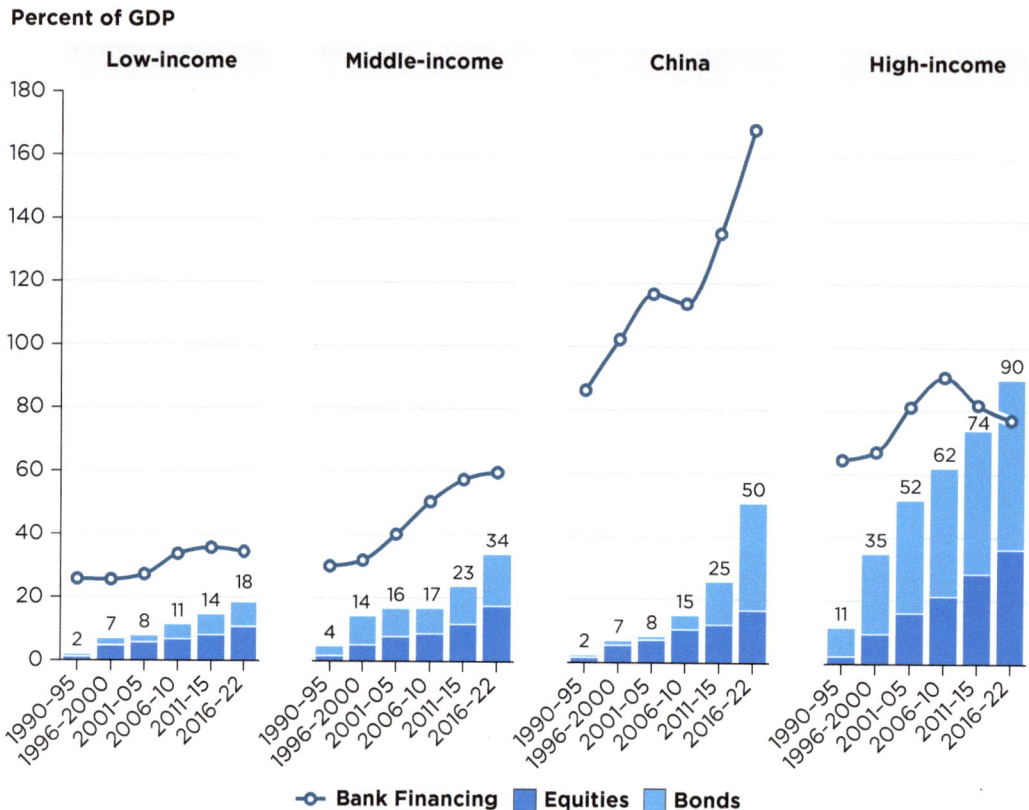

Percent of GDP

Sources: Calculations using issuance data from the Securities Data Company Platinum database from LSEG and GDP and bank claims data from the World Bank's World Development Indicators.

Note: Bank claims represent outstanding domestic credit to the private sector. For capital markets, the figure presents the cumulative net amount of bond and equity issuance (as a percentage of GDP) for financial and nonfinancial firms for 1990–2022. CNI as a ratio to GDP for year *Y* is computed as the sum of equity issuance, bond issuance (minus bonds that matured), or both between 1990 and year *Y*, divided by GDP in year *Y*. The figure reports five-year averages (except for 1990–95 and 2016–22, where it reports six-year and seven-year averages, respectively) for such ratios. Outstanding bank loans to the private sector include pre-1990 bank loans. Bank claims as a ratio of GDP for year *Y* are calculated as bank claims for year *Y* divided by GDP in year *Y*. The figure reports the average of such ratios across years in each subsample. Appendix B provides the list of countries, grouped by income category. CNI = cumulative net capital issuance; GDP = gross domestic product.

To learn more about the patterns of bond and equity issuances by nonfinancial firms in domestic and foreign capital markets, this book uses novel transaction- and firm-level data. It focuses on firms that have raised funds via bond or equity issuances in capital markets, and it emphasizes developments in low- and middle-income countries. Drawing on this information, the book explores the implications of the findings for firm performance and aggregate economic activity, providing insights about firm financing worldwide and the policy actions that can spur capital market development.

Capital market activity is integral to economic and financial development. Although firms participating in capital markets are a small fraction of the total number of firms in an economy, they usually account for a large share of national income.[5] Moreover, developments in capital markets and participating firms also affect businesses that rely exclusively on alternative sources of financing, such as bank credit or private equity. For example, capital market financing for large corporations can free up resources for smaller firms, easing credit constraints. This improved financing might be available directly through network linkages to issuing firms or indirectly as banks reallocate credit across the economy. Enhanced capital markets activity may also influence private equity by improving exit opportunities, making such investments more attractive. Moreover, nonparticipating firms could also be striving to gain access to capital markets. Understanding the attributes and behaviors of firms that secure financing, such as how they invest and grow, has implications for aggregate economic outcomes and could ultimately help to identify opportunities for nonparticipating firms.

This understanding is especially important for low- and middle-income countries. As shown in the data set used in the book, during the 1990s, the number of firms in low- and middle-income countries that were issuing on capital markets was around a quarter of the number in high-income countries (figure 1.2). However, activity has increased significantly since then, driven by new participants (firms that had no issuance activity prior to 2000). Among these new participants, the number of firms in low- and middle-income countries is now half the number of firms in high-income countries. Perhaps more important, in 2000–22, new participants accounted for the majority of issuances in low- and middle-income countries, whereas firms that had been active in the 1990s still constituted the largest share of issuances in high-income countries. Recognizing the potential of such increased activity, the book examines the characteristics of firms that are accessing capital markets, their growth after issuance, and the implications of these dynamics for the wider economy.

FIGURE 1.2

New Participants Dominate Issuance Activity in Low- and
Middle-Income Countries After 2000

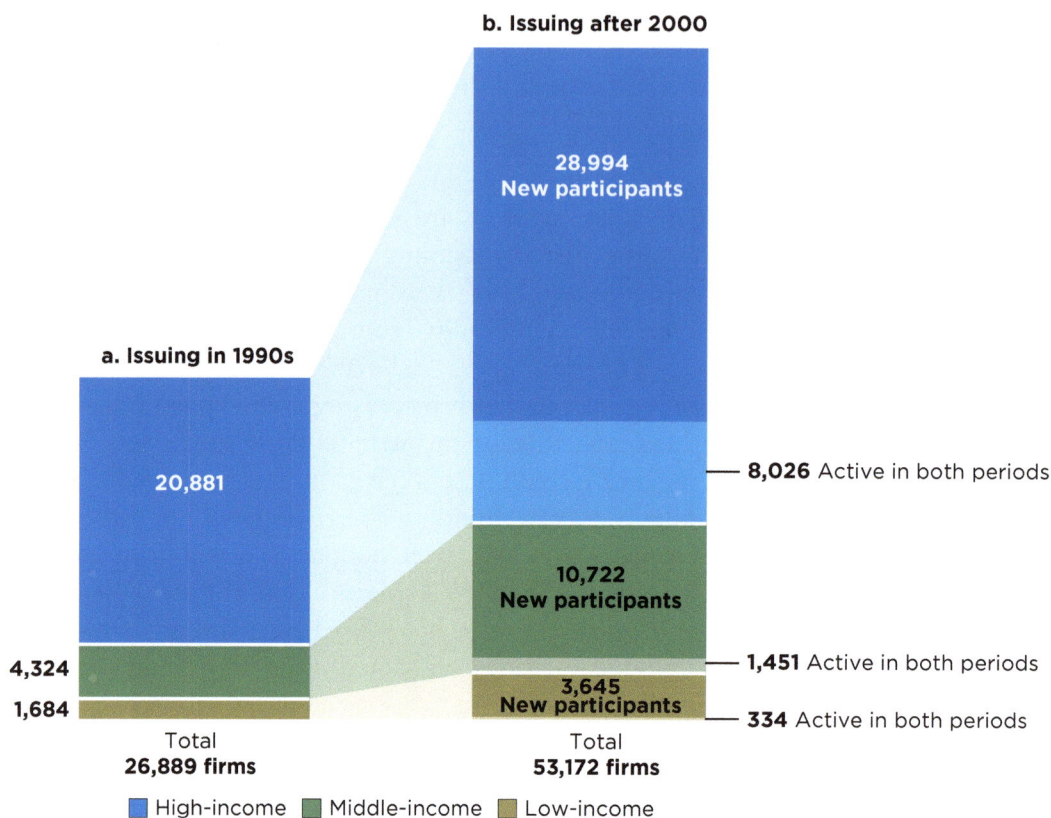

b. Issuing after 2000

28,994
New participants

a. Issuing in 1990s

20,881

——— **8,026** Active in both periods

10,722
New participants

4,324

——— **1,451** Active in both periods

1,684

3,645
New participants

——— **334** Active in both periods

Total
26,889 firms

Total
53,172 firms

■ High-income ■ Middle-income ■ Low-income

Source: Calculations using issuance data from the Securities Data Company Platinum database from LSEG.
Note: The bars in panel a display the number of firms with issuance activity in capital markets between 1990 and 1999, categorized by country income group. The bars in panel b show the number of firms with issuance activity between 2000 and 2022, distinguishing between firms that issued in both the 1990–99 and the 2000–22 periods, and new participants—those that issued for the first time from 2000 onward. Appendix B provides the list of countries, grouped by income category. The figure does not include China.

An overarching theme of the book is that the number of firms accessing capital markets is increasing in an expanding range of countries, with the total volume of financing in low- and middle-income countries steadily converging toward the volume in high-income countries. Although this trend is driven partly by faster economic growth in many low- and middle-income countries in recent decades, it raises the question of which policy measures have been effective in strengthening capital markets. By connecting issuance data with various financial sector policies across countries, the book identifies measures that may expand the supply of financing and facilitate its efficient allocation to firms.

By examining firms that raised funds through capital markets, the analysis captures relatively large firms within each country. For instance, among low- and middle-income countries, the median firm in the sample has annual sales of approximately US$70 million, employs more than 700 workers, and raises US$16 million per issuance.[6] Therefore, in this book, references to firm characteristics and their behavior over time generally pertain to the firms that access capital markets. The analysis does not cover the millions of smaller firms that do not access capital market financing at all, but instead rely primarily on bank credit, private equity, trade finance, or other sources of finance.

FIGURE 1.3

The Conceptual Framework Connects Capital Markets with Firm Performance and Economic Outcomes

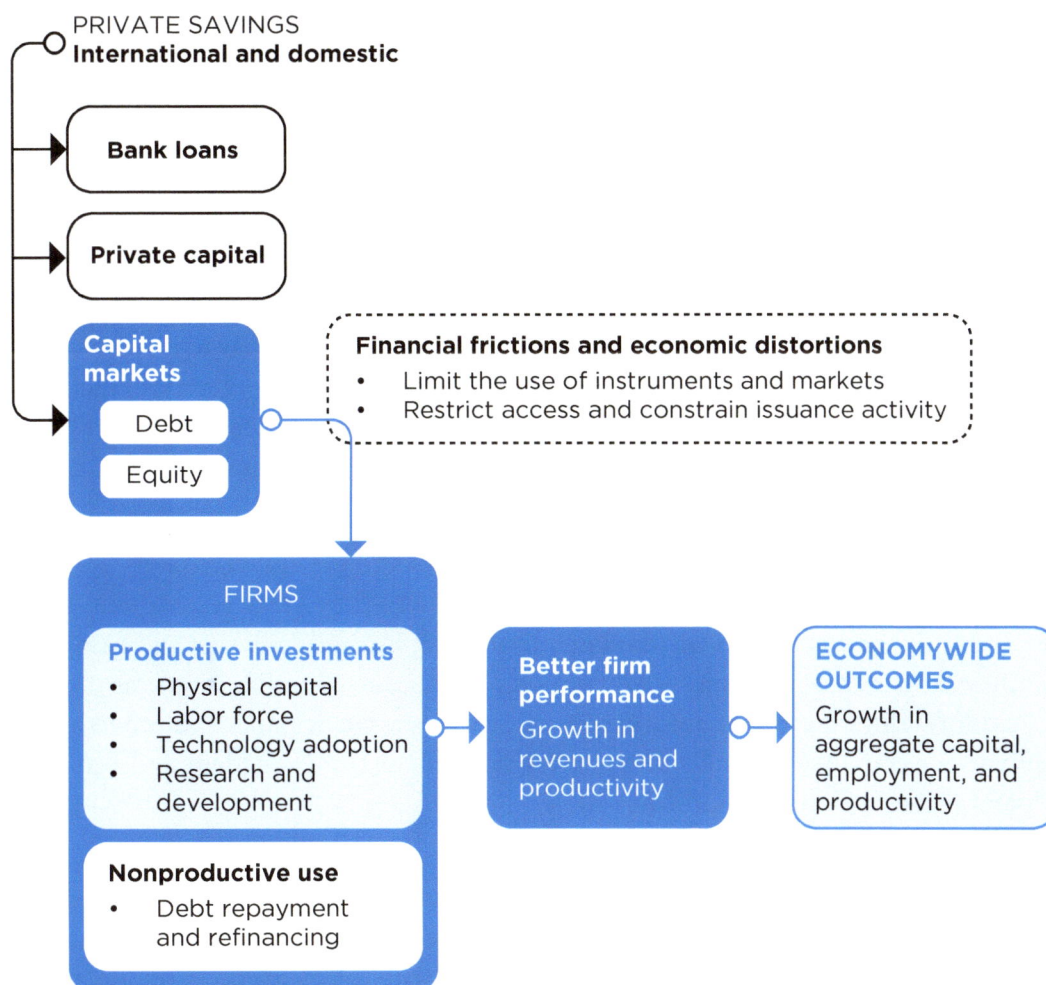

Sources: International Finance Corporation and the World Bank.

A simple conceptual framework connecting capital market financing to firm performance and economywide growth and productivity guides the discussion (figure 1.3). The impact of the additional capital market financing on firm performance depends critically on whether firms use the new funds to augment their physical capital and labor force, invest in technology adoption and research and development, and undertake innovation or whether they merely accumulate cash or alter their liabilities—by adjusting debt-equity ratios or replacing more expensive financing with cheaper funding. The answers are not obvious ex ante, so the book analyzes how firms allocate the new funds.

What Are the Book's Main Contributions?

Previous studies have analyzed various aspects of capital markets (for example, refer to Carvajal et al. 2019; CGFS 2019; Didier et al. 2021; Pagano, Panetta, and Zingales 1998; World Bank 2017, 2020; appendix A offers a review). For low- and middle-income countries, however, the coverage across regions has been uneven. It is important to understand which firms in these countries tap domestic and international capital markets, what the modalities of their financing are, and how access to capital markets affects their performance and aggregate economic outcomes. The book analyzes the following issues:

- *Granular trends in capital market financing in low- and middle-income countries over 1990–2022.* The book goes beyond aggregate metrics of market size to examine the types of financing instruments and the characteristics of firms accessing these markets, covering both domestic and foreign issuances. It also breaks down capital market financing for firms that were active issuers before 2000 and new participants after 2000 to understand how the composition of issuers has evolved.

- *Firm growth after fundraising activity.* To understand the real effects of participation in capital markets, the book examines how firms in low- and middle-income countries accumulate physical capital and how they increase their employment and sales following new issuance activity. The book further explores differing effects across types of firms (new participants and others), issuance activity (first and subsequent issuances), instruments (debt and equity), and markets (domestic and foreign).

- *Impact on capital allocation and aggregate economic outcomes.* The book estimates the gains in aggregate productivity when firms obtain financing from capital markets. It applies several techniques to connect firm-level observables to efficiency gains from having access to capital markets. This approach attempts to gauge the effects of such financing on aggregate capital stock, employment, and productivity.

- *Drivers and policies supporting capital market expansion.* The book analyzes several policy measures intended to foster the growth of capital markets in low- and middle-income countries. These measures include developing domestic institutional investors, implementing international capital account liberalization measures, establishing a sovereign bond market to serve as a price benchmark, strengthening investor protection, and improving the information environment. By linking issuance data with these policies, the book points to possible avenues for policy makers to promote capital market development and for firms to gain access to these markets.

The book also introduces an interactive online tool—the Capital Markets Portal, which is available at https://capitalmarketsportal.worldbank.org—for exploring recent trends in capital market financing and estimating their impact on aggregate economic outcomes.[7] Beyond reproducing the results documented here, readers can also explore and compare findings for additional subsets of regions and countries.

The book is organized as follows. Chapters 2 and 3 describe in depth the data on capital market activity, gaining insights into the growth of issuance activity by firms, countries, and markets. These chapters examine the extent of growth across different dimensions—such as debt versus equity or domestic versus foreign markets—and explore the patterns of capital market expansion at various levels of disaggregation. Chapter 2 explores the expansion of capital markets across countries, while chapter 3 investigates the expansion of capital markets across firms, differentiating between new participants and others.[8]

Chapter 4 focuses on the impact of these observed patterns in capital market financing on firm and aggregate growth. It examines changes in firms' physical capital, employment, and sales resulting from issuance activity. It also quantifies the implications for aggregate productivity growth, while identifying types of firms and regions where capital markets generate the largest impact.

Chapter 5 ties these findings to the drivers—including policies—of the documented expansion of capital markets in low- and middle-income countries. It discusses potential measures that policy makers and firms can take to increase capital market financing in these countries. It concludes by proposing a research agenda to advance the development of capital markets in low- and middle-income countries, building on the findings.

Notes

1. For a review of studies on the impact of capital market financing on growth, refer to Carvajal et al. (2019).

2. Capital market finance also poses some risk, but such analysis is outside the scope of this book. On occasion, excessive reliance on and expansion of financing can contribute to economic and financial volatility, as evidenced, for example, by the buildup to the global financial crisis beginning in 2008 (Sahay et al. 2015).

3. Because of its large size and shift from low-income to middle-income status during the sample period, China is excluded from both low- and middle-income categories and is presented separately throughout the book, unless noted otherwise.

4. Another way to compare the size of the banking sector with that of capital markets is by focusing on market capitalization as a share of GDP. However, this commonly used measure reflects both the effects of valuation and the direct financing of firms through security issuances. Still, with this caveat in mind, capital markets look sizable when focusing on market capitalization. In low- and middle-income countries, the market capitalization of stocks alone is comparable to the outstanding claims of banks on the private sector. This finding underscores the importance of studying the financing that capital markets provide to firms in low- and middle-income countries.

5. Firms participating in capital markets belong to a range of sectors. In low- and middle-income countries, the largest share of firms operate in the manufacturing (51 percent), services (15 percent), and transportation and communications (14 percent) sectors. Not all firms issuing in capital markets are publicly listed; 48 percent remained privately owned throughout the sample period (1990–2022). See appendix C for more details on the distribution of firms across sectors and type of ownership.

6. Employment data are available only for a subset of publicly listed firms, typically the largest within this group.

7. The Capital Markets Portal can be accessed at https://capitalmarketsportal.worldbank.org.

8. About a quarter of the firms worldwide in the sample are from low- and middle-income countries (7 percent from low-income countries and 19 percent from middle-income countries; firms in China and high-income countries constitute 12 percent and 62 percent, respectively).

References

Carvajal, A., R. Bebczuk, A. C. Silva, and A. G. Mora. 2019. *Capital Markets Development: Causes, Effects, and Sequencing*. Washington, DC: World Bank. https://documents .worldbank.org/en/publication/documents-reports/documentdetail/701021588343376548 /capital-markets-development-causes-effects-and-sequencing.

CGFS (Committee on the Global Financial System). 2019. "Establishing Viable Capital Markets." CGFS Paper 62, Bank for International Settlements, Basel, Switzerland. https://www.bis.org/publ/cgfs62.pdf.

Didier, T., R. Levine, R. L. Montanes, and S. L. Schmukler. 2021. "Capital Market Financing and Firm Growth." *Journal of International Money and Finance* 118 (July): 102459. https://doi.org/10.1016/j.jimonfin.2021.102459.

Pagano, M., F. Panetta, and L. Zingales. 1998. "Why Do Companies Go Public? An Empirical Analysis." *Journal of Finance* 53 (1): 27–64. https://doi.org/10.1111/0022-1082.25448.

Sahay, R., M. Cihak, P. M. N'Diaye, A. Barajas, R. Bi, D. Ayala, Y. Gao, A. Kyobe, L. Nguyen, C. Saborowski, K. Svirydzenka, and S. R. Yousefi. 2015. *Rethinking Financial Deepening: Stability and Growth in Emerging Markets*. Washington, DC: International Monetary Fund.

World Bank. 2017. *Promoting the Use of Capital Markets for Infrastructure Financing: Lessons for Securities Markets Regulators in Emerging Market Economies*. Washington, DC: World Bank.

World Bank. 2020. *Capital Markets Development: A Primer for Policymakers*. Washington, DC: World Bank.

CHAPTER 2

Expansion of Capital Markets Globally

Pablo Hernando-Kaminsky

Key Messages

- Cumulative net capital issuance (CNI) by firms in low- and middle-income countries amounted to approximately US$4 trillion in 1990–2022, compared with US$34 trillion by all firms globally (in constant 2020 US dollars).

- The period between 2000 and 2022 witnessed a fourfold increase in capital market financing in middle-income countries and an eightfold increase in low-income countries.

- CNI grew from 2 percent of gross domestic product (GDP) in 1990–99 to 8 percent in 2010–22 in low-income countries and from 5 percent to 17 percent in middle-income countries.

- In the 1990s, firms from 38 high-income countries, 47 middle-income countries, 14 low-income countries, and China issued equity or bonds in capital markets. Between 2000 and 2022, firms from 32 additional middle-income countries and 13 additional low-income countries gained access to capital markets.

- Both capital market financing and the number of issuing firms grew strongly in all geographic regions, especially in low- and middle-income countries.

- In China, annual CNI rose from 3 percent of GDP, on average, in 1990–99 to 20 percent of GDP in 2010–22, against the backdrop of rapid GDP growth.

- Bonds and equities contributed roughly equal proportions to total CNI across all income groups, except in low-income countries, where equities accounted for two-thirds.

- Domestic market issuance accounted for more than half of the total in low- and middle-income countries (79 percent of equity and 53 percent of bonds during 1990–2022).

Capital Market Activity Has Surged for Firms Both Globally and within Low- and Middle-Income Countries

Global CNI (starting in 1990 as the base year) for nonfinancial firms was around US$10 trillion by end-1999 and US$34 trillion by end-2022 (figure 2.1, panel a), with low- and middle-income countries accounting for US$4 trillion by 2022 (all data are in constant 2020 US dollars).[1]

Whereas capital markets were relatively small for low- and middle-income countries in the 1990s and early 2000s,[2] they have since made significant strides, with CNI up about eightfold in low-income countries and fourfold in middle-income countries from the late 1990s to 2022 (figure 2.1, panels b and c).[3] China mirrored the trajectory of low-income countries until the late 2000s, but its CNI subsequently surged, with a more than fourfold increase from 2010 to 2022 (figure 2.1, panel d). As for high-income countries, their CNI increased threefold from the late 1990s to 2022 (figure 2.1, panel e).

FIGURE 2.1

CNI for Nonfinancial Firms Grew Rapidly in 1990–2022 Worldwide and within Low- and Middle-Income Countries

Billions of constant 2020 US dollars

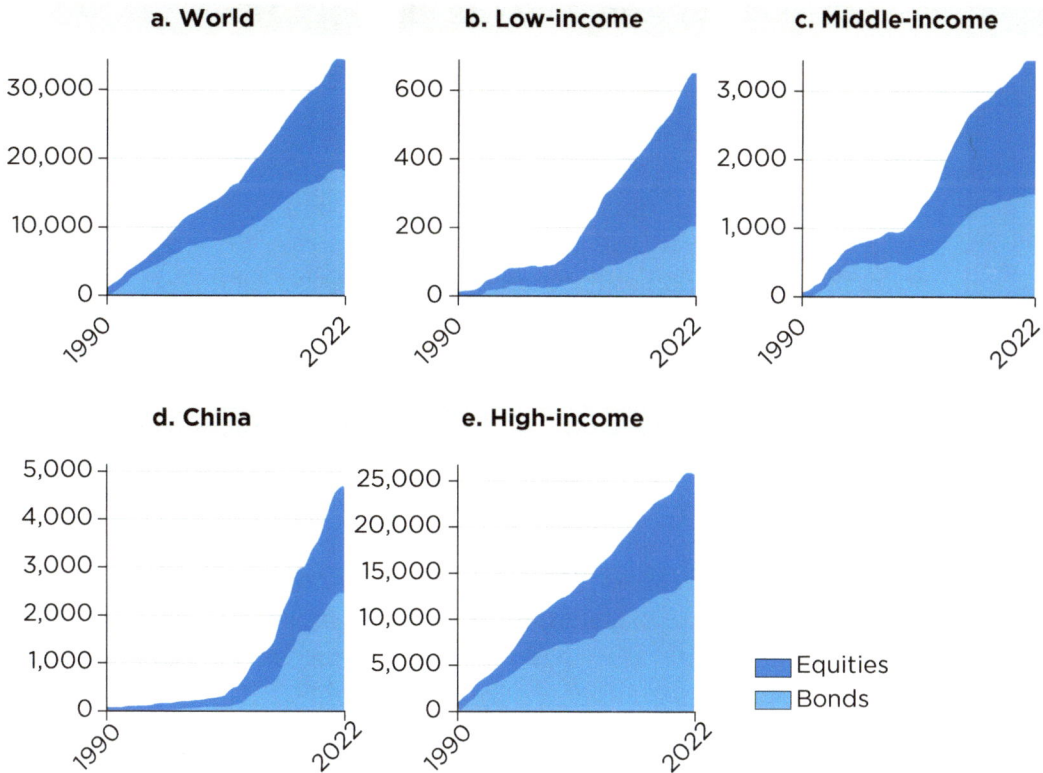

Source: Calculations using issuance data from the Securities Data Company Platinum database from LSEG.

Note: This figure presents the CNI of bond and equity issuance for nonfinancial firms in 1990–2022 in billions of constant 2020 US dollars. CNI for year *Y* is computed as the sum of equity issuance and bond issuance (minus bonds that matured) between 1990 and year *Y*. Appendix B provides the list of countries, grouped by income category. CNI = cumulative net capital issuance.

Box 2.1 describes the data used for this analysis.

BOX 2.1

Data on CNI Facilitate an Understanding of Capital Markets Worldwide

The primary database used is the Securities Data Company Platinum database from LSEG, which offers extensive data on new bond issues, mergers and acquisitions, syndicated loans, and equity.[a] This book leverages data on capital issuances for both publicly listed and privately held companies for the 1990–2022 period. Detailed transaction-level information from the Securities Data Company Platinum database provides comprehensive coverage of global bond and equity issuances, facilitating a thorough documentation and characterization of capital markets worldwide and yielding detailed insights into the participation of countries and firms. Although the Securities Data Company Platinum database includes data on issuance by financial firms and governments, this book primarily analyzes issuance by nonfinancial firms.[b] While issuances by governments and government agencies are excluded from the data set, state-owned enterprises (defined as firms with direct state ownership of 50 percent or more) are included (see appendix C for more details).

The book focuses on cumulative net capital issuance (CNI), which—for each period under consideration—is calculated as the sum of equity and bond issuances since 1990 minus bonds that have matured since 1990.[c] For example, CNI over 1990–2022 is the sum of all issuances of equities and bonds, minus bond redemptions, during that period. It is termed "cumulative" because it sums all capital issued since the start of the period and "net" because matured bonds are subtracted. For long periods, using a cumulative measure has similarities to analyzing the stock of financing, such as outstanding bank credit. Furthermore, CNI is not distorted by the refinancing of bond debt, capturing instead only additional financing to firms.[d]

Equity has no maturity date and hence is not subtracted from CNI. On occasion, firms may reduce their outstanding equities by

continued

BOX 2.1 *(Continued)*

buying them back through transactions known as stock buybacks. In this book, such transactions are not considered, owing to data limitations. However, existing evidence shows that this approach yields an acceptable approximation, especially for low- and middle-income countries. In 2022, global stock buybacks accounted for only 3.6 percent of global CNI and occurred primarily in high-income countries (Manconi, Peyer, and Vermaelen 2019).

a. Appendix C presents a more detailed overview of the data and data coverage, while appendix B presents the countries included in the book.

b. Appendix D reviews financial firm issuance and compares it to nonfinancial firm issuance.

c. The sample period begins in 1990 given the incomplete coverage of country capital issuance data before that year. Therefore, CNI is set to zero at the start of the year 1990 for the purpose of this book's analysis. Of course, capital markets predate this period—for example, stock market capitalization amounted to approximately US$19 trillion by 1990 (appendix E).

d. An alternative measure of capital market activity is gross capital issuance—the volume of bonds and equity issued each year. As opposed to net issuance, gross issuance for bonds includes maturing bonds that are being rolled over (representing refinancing rather than additional financing for a firm). Appendix F discusses gross issuance, finding that bonds represent a majority (72 percent) of gross capital issued each year.

Low- and Middle-Income Countries' Share of Global Capital Market Financing Is Rising

Starting from a low base in 1990, the share of global CNI by low- and middle-income countries rose rapidly in the mid-1990s and again in the mid-2000s (figure 2.2). By 2022, this share had grown to 12 percent.

FIGURE 2.2

Low- and Middle-Income Countries Increased Their Share of
Global Capital Markets between 1990 and 2022

Percent of global CNI

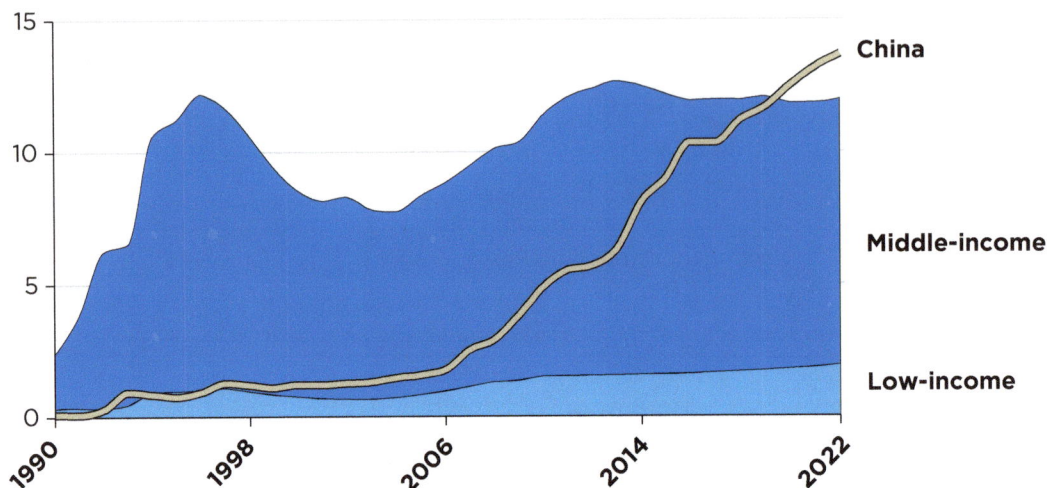

Source: Calculations using issuance data from the Securities Data Company Platinum
database from LSEG.
Note: This figure presents the annual share of global CNI accounted for by middle-
income countries, low-income countries, and China. CNI for year *Y* is computed as the
sum of equity issuance and bond issuance (minus bonds that matured) between 1990
and year *Y*. Appendix B provides the list of countries, grouped by income category.
CNI = cumulative net capital issuance.

The share of middle-income countries in capital markets rose the most in the
1990s, followed by a slight decline in the early 2000s, which subsequently
rebounded in the late 2000s and has since stabilized at around 10 percent. Capital
markets in low-income countries have grown steadily over the past 30 years.
Although still modest (approximately 2 percent by 2022), their share of global CNI
was more than twice as large as it was at the end of the 1990s. China followed
a growth trajectory similar to that of low-income countries until the late 2000s,
surging thereafter from 5 percent of the total in 2010 to 13 percent in 2022.

Cumulative Net Capital Issuance Has Risen Faster Than GDP

CNI outpaced GDP both at the global level and in each group of countries
considered during the past three decades (figure 2.3). In 1990–99, annual CNI as
a share of global GDP was, on average, 9 percent.[4] By 2010–22, it amounted to
32 percent. Similar trends are observed when examining solely low- and middle-
income countries.[5] In low-income countries, it grew from 2 percent of GDP in

1990–99 to 8 percent in 2010–22, while in middle-income countries, it increased from 5 percent to 17 percent. Particularly notable is China, whose capital relative to GDP grew more than sixfold over the three decades. In high-income countries, issuance rose from 10 percent of GDP in 1990–99 to 43 percent in 2010–22, outpacing the more modest economic growth experienced by this group of countries.

FIGURE 2.3

Growth in CNI Outpaced Growth in GDP, 1990–2022

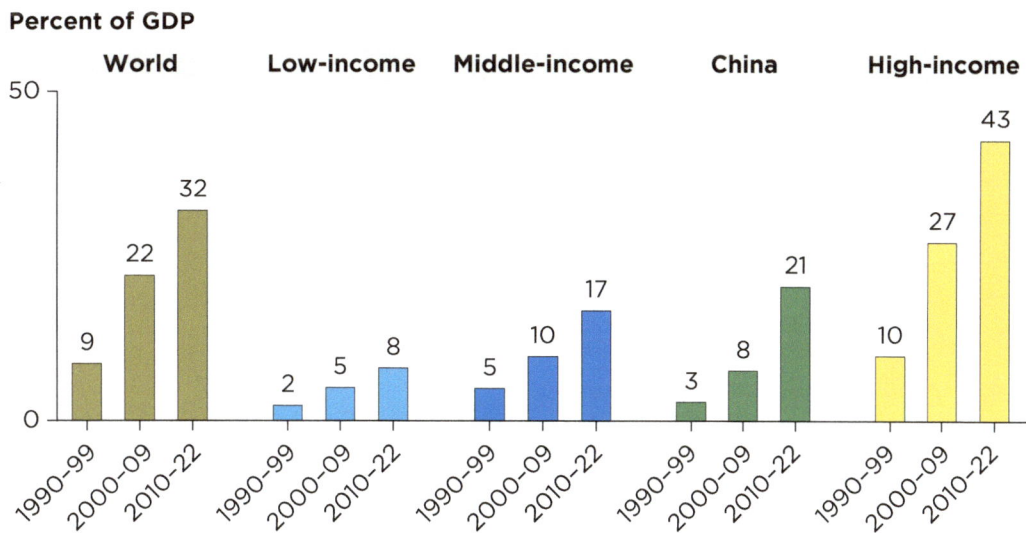

Percent of GDP

Sources: Calculations using issuance data from the Securities Data Company Platinum database from LSEG and GDP data from the World Bank's World Development Indicators. *Note:* This figure presents the CNI (as a percentage of GDP) for nonfinancial firms for 1990–2022. CNI as a ratio to GDP for year *Y* is computed as the sum of equity issuance and bond issuance (minus bonds that matured) between 1990 and year *Y*, divided by GDP in year *Y*. The figure reports decade averages for such ratios. Appendix B provides the list of countries, grouped by income category. CNI = cumulative net capital issuance; GDP = gross domestic product.

Among low- and middle-income countries, East Asia and Pacific led in CNI as a percentage of GDP across all three decades: 11 percent in 1990–99, 20 percent in 2000–09, and more than 25 percent in 2010–22. However, growth was evident in low- and middle-income countries in other regions as well (figure 2.4). Latin America and the Caribbean reached about 20 percent of GDP in 2010–22. The Middle East and North Africa and Sub-Saharan Africa regions, which had minimal access to capital markets in 1990–99, experienced a remarkable financial market expansion over the past two decades. CNI in the Middle East and North Africa started at 0.15 percent of GDP in 1990–99 and rose to 4 percent of GDP in 2010–22. Capital market growth was also robust in Sub-Saharan Africa, with CNI reaching around 6 percent of GDP in 2010–22.

FIGURE 2.4

CNI Rose for All Low- and Middle-Income Regions between
1990 and 2022

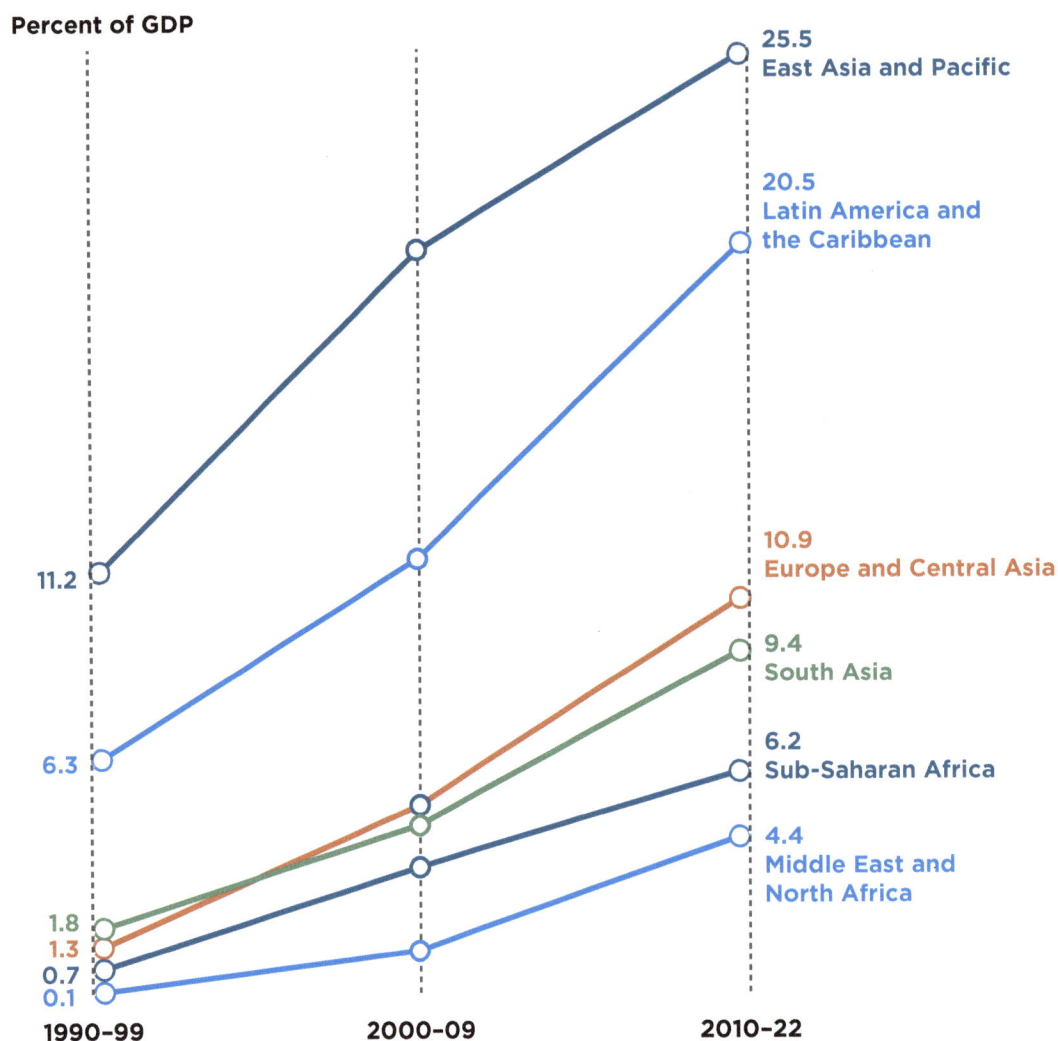

Percent of GDP

25.5
East Asia and Pacific

20.5
**Latin America and
the Caribbean**

10.9
Europe and Central Asia

9.4
South Asia

6.2
Sub-Saharan Africa

4.4
**Middle East and
North Africa**

11.2

6.3

1.8
1.3
0.7
0.1

1990–99   **2000–09**   **2010–22**

Sources: Calculations using issuance data are from the Securities Data Company
Platinum database from LSEG and GDP data from the World Bank's World Development
Indicators.
Note: This figure shows the average CNI (as a percentage of GDP) across decades
for low- and middle-income countries by region. CNI as a ratio to GDP for year *Y* is
computed as the sum of equity issuance and bond issuance (minus bonds that matured)
between 1990 and year *Y*, divided by GDP in year *Y*. The figure reports decade averages
for such ratios. Appendix B provides the list of countries, grouped by income category.
CNI = cumulative net capital issuance; GDP = gross domestic product.

Firms in More Countries Are Tapping Capital Markets

From 1990 to 2022, firms in 147 countries accessed capital markets, including 106 low- and middle-income countries.[6] Of these countries, 47 had zero CNI in 1990–99. Firms in these countries (32 middle-income, 13 low-income, and 2 high-income countries) gained access to capital markets between 2000 and 2022 (map 2.1).[7] The majority of these new market entrants are in Africa and the Middle East. Three countries had zero issuance in 2010–22, after experiencing positive issuance in 1990–2009 (map 2.1).[8]

MAP 2.1

Firms in 32 More Middle-Income Countries and in 13 More Low-Income Countries Entered Capital Markets between 2000 and 2022

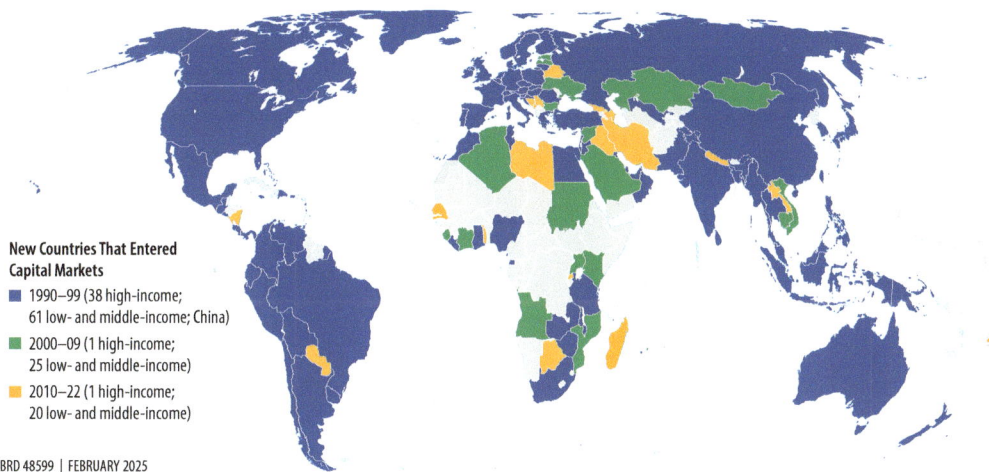

New Countries That Entered Capital Markets
- 1990–99 (38 high-income; 61 low- and middle-income; China)
- 2000–09 (1 high-income; 25 low- and middle-income)
- 2010–22 (1 high-income; 20 low- and middle-income)

IBRD 48599 | FEBRUARY 2025

Source: Calculations using issuance data from the Securities Data Company Platinum database from LSEG.
Note: This map reports the timing of issuance for firms in each country. A single bond or equity issuance qualifies a country to be counted as having capital market activity. Although firms were able to issue in capital markets, the activity in several countries might be limited. Appendix B provides the list of countries, grouped by income category.

Firms in a growing number of countries have tapped capital markets over the past 30 years, and the amount of CNI for each country has increased as well. In 1990–99, CNI was less than 2 percent of GDP in more than half of countries in the sample (figure 2.5). In contrast, by 2010–22, CNI was less than 2 percent of GDP in less than a third of the countries. The shifts to the right show that capital market issuance has become larger for most countries. Overall, more firms in more countries have begun to participate in capital markets and to access larger amounts of capital.

FIGURE 2.5

Firms in More Countries Accessed Capital Markets, and CNI
Increased in Most Countries between 1990 and 2022

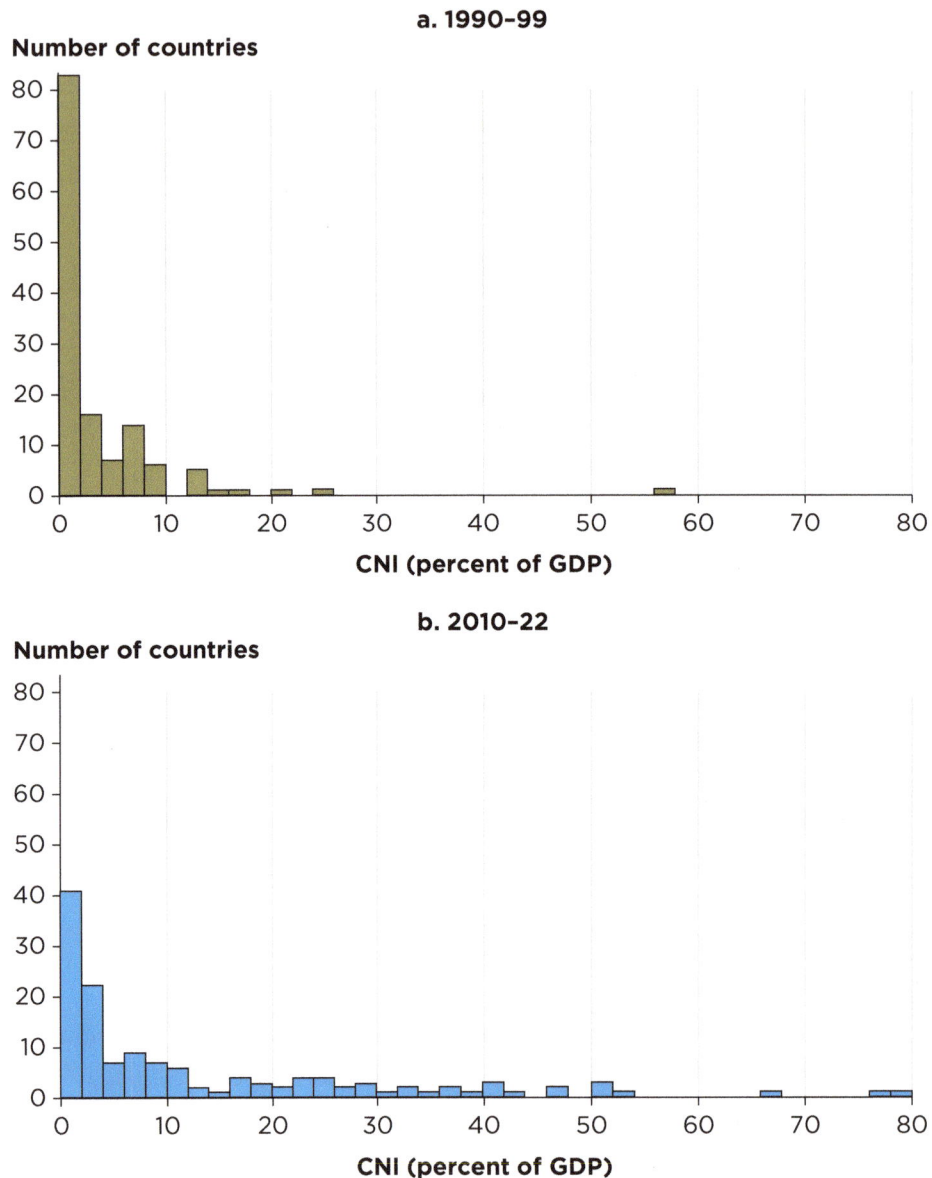

a. 1990–99

Number of countries

CNI (percent of GDP)

b. 2010–22

Number of countries

CNI (percent of GDP)

Sources: Calculations using issuance data from the Securities Data Company Platinum
database from LSEG and GDP data from the World Bank's World Development Indicators.
Note: This figure compares the first decade with the last decade in the sample period
considered. It presents the histogram of CNI (as a percentage of GDP) for 1990–99
and 2010–22, for all countries. CNI as a ratio to GDP for year *Y* is computed as the
sum of equity issuance and bond issuance (minus bonds that matured) between
1990 and year *Y*, divided by GDP in year *Y*. The figure reports decade averages for
such ratios. Appendix B provides the list of countries, grouped by income category.
CNI = cumulative net capital issuance; GDP = gross domestic product.

Bonds and Equities Contribute Roughly Equal Proportions to Total Cumulative Net Capital Issuance, Except in Low-Income Countries

Firms must weigh various financial and strategic factors when deciding whether to issue bonds or equity. Bonds impose fixed financial obligations, and although interest payments are tax deductible, they can restrict cash flow. In contrast, equity does not involve regular payments and thus offers greater flexibility, but it dilutes ownership, which may be unappealing to existing shareholders. Market conditions also influence this decision-making process. Favorable interest rates and credit markets may make bond issuance more attractive, whereas strong stock market conditions and high company valuations might prompt a firm to issue equity.

Initially, bonds constituted the majority of CNI in middle-income countries, at 56 percent in the 1990s (figure 2.6, panel b). By 2022, however, CNI was slightly more than half the total, comparable to that in high-income countries.[9] For low-income countries, equity consistently outweighed bonds, accounting for three-quarters of total CNI, on average, over the entire period (figure 2.6, panel a).[10] This pattern was also evident in China in 1990–99 and 2000–09, but from 2010 onward, China's bonds surged, rising from around 5 percent of GDP in 2010 to around 15 percent by 2022 (figure 2.6, panel c). Although equity continued to increase after 2010, China's bonds became the main driver of capital growth, and by 2022, bonds and equity contributed roughly equal proportions to CNI.

FIGURE 2.6

Bonds and Equities Accounted for Equivalent Shares of CNI in Middle- and High-Income Countries, whereas Equities Prevailed in Low-Income Countries

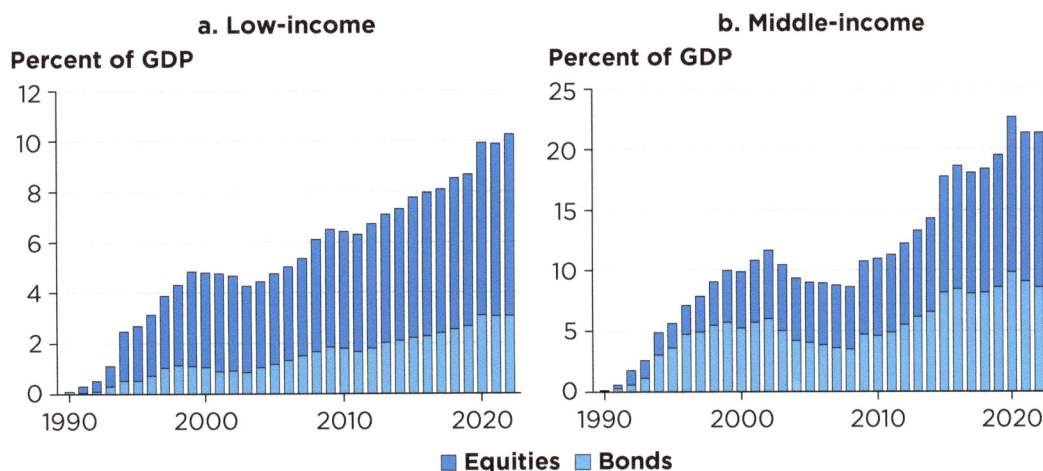

a. Low-income
Percent of GDP

b. Middle-income
Percent of GDP

■ Equities ■ Bonds

continued

FIGURE 2.6 *(Continued)*

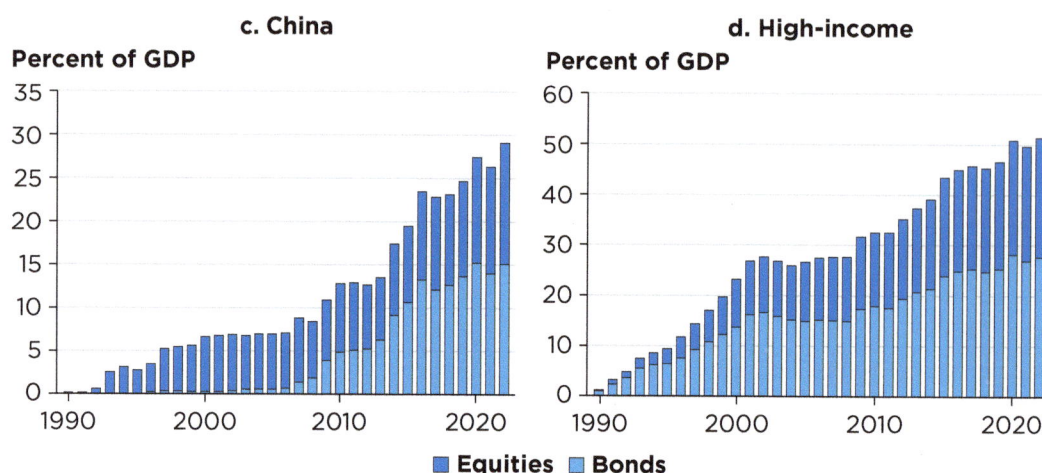

c. China

Percent of GDP

d. High-income

Percent of GDP

■ Equities ■ Bonds

Sources: Calculations using issuance data from the Securities Data Company Platinum database from LSEG and GDP data from the World Bank's World Development Indicators.

Note: This figure presents CNI of bonds and equities (as a percentage of GDP). CNI as a ratio to GDP for year *Y* is computed as the sum of equity issuance and bond issuance (minus bonds that matured) between 1990 and year *Y*, divided by GDP in year *Y*. Appendix B provides the list of countries, grouped by income category. CNI = cumulative net capital issuance; GDP = gross domestic product.

Issuance Is More Prominent in Domestic Capital Markets Than in International Markets

Firms consider several factors when deciding whether to raise capital in domestic or in international capital markets. In domestic markets, firms typically are better known to domestic investors and financial analysts, which can boost investor confidence and facilitate access to funding. However, these markets may be limited in the amount of capital that can be raised. For firms needing large amounts of capital, international markets provide access to a larger pool of investors with sizable funds. In addition, international markets often attract a diverse set of investors, including institutional investors. This diversity can enhance liquidity and potentially result in more favorable terms for raising capital. However, firms seeking capital may need to disclose more information in international markets than in domestic markets.

Currency also influences the choice of market. When issuing in international markets, firms whose revenues are in local currency will usually face currency risk because capital raised is typically in foreign currency.[11] If a firm issues a bond in a foreign currency and its local currency depreciates against the financing currency, the amount to be repaid in local currency increases. Conversely, domestic market issuance is usually in local currency, which mitigates risk. Ultimately, the choice between domestic and international markets depends on balancing these factors to align with the firm's strategic goals and financial needs.[12]

In the analysis that follows, bond issuances are defined as domestic or international by comparing the market location of issuance with the residence of the issuing firm.[13] Similarly, equity is classified as domestic or international by comparing the location of the primary exchange where a firm's stock trades with the residence of the issuing firm.

Most of the growth of capital markets in low- and middle-income countries occurred in domestic markets, which accounted for 79 percent of equity and 53 percent of bond cumulative net issuances between 1990 and 2022 (figure 2.7 presents data for low- and middle-income countries separately). China displayed minimal reliance on international capital, with only 8 percent of equity and 5 percent of bonds being issued in international markets in 2022.

FIGURE 2.7

Domestic Capital Markets Drove the Growth of CNI between 1990 and 2022

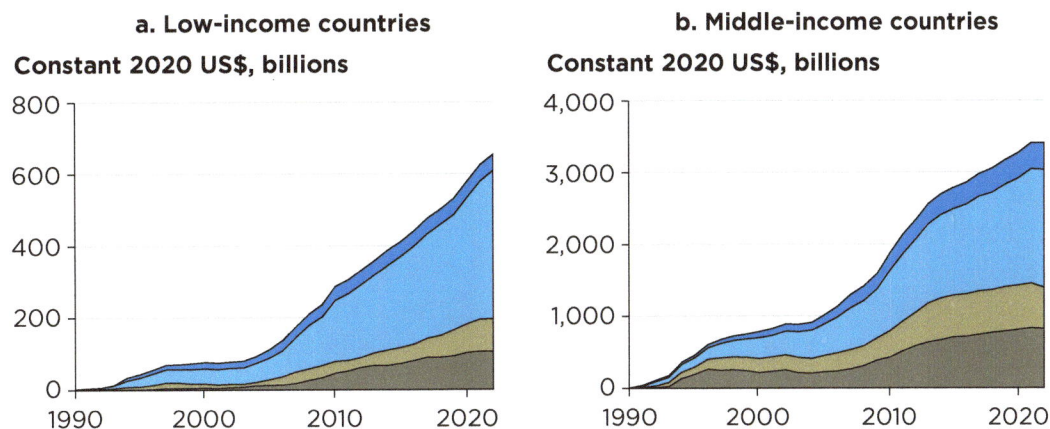

a. Low-income countries
Constant 2020 US$, billions

b. Middle-income countries
Constant 2020 US$, billions

continued

FIGURE 2.7 *(Continued)*

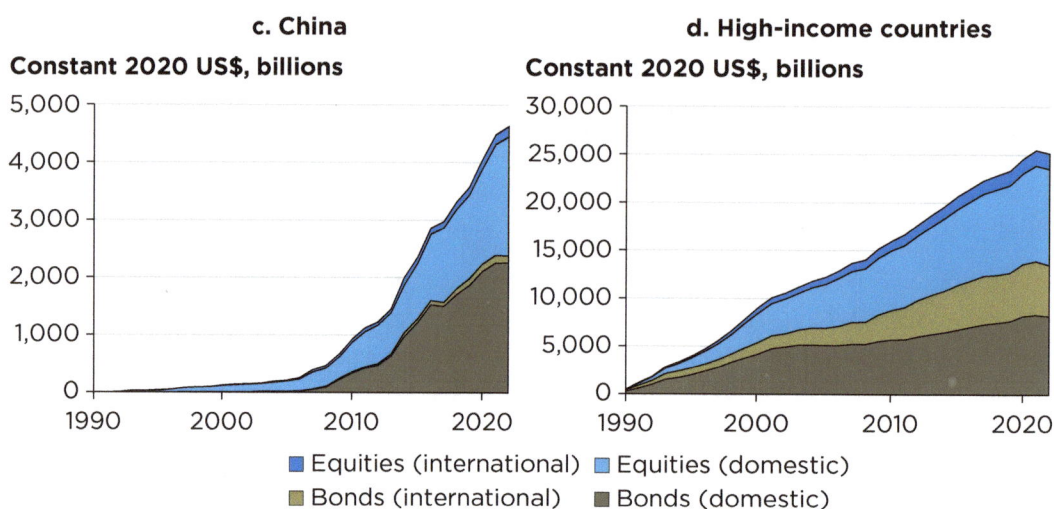

c. China
Constant 2020 US$, billions

d. High-income countries
Constant 2020 US$, billions

Equities (international) Equities (domestic)
Bonds (international) Bonds (domestic)

Source: Calculations using issuance data from the Securities Data Company Platinum database from LSEG.

Note: This figure presents the amount of CNI in domestic and international markets for 1990–2022 in billions of constant 2020 US dollars. CNI for year *Y* is computed as the sum of equity issuance and bond issuance (minus bonds that matured) between 1990 and year *Y*. Bonds are categorized as domestic or international by comparing the market location of issuance with the residence of the issuing firm. Equity is classified as domestic or international by comparing the location of the primary exchange where a firm's stock trades with the residence of the issuing firm. Appendix B provides the list of countries, grouped by income category. CNI = cumulative net capital issuance; GDP = gross domestic product.

In low- and middle-income countries, the share of domestic CNI rose from about 63 percent in 1990–99 to 70 percent in 2010–22 (figure 2.7, panel a), and in high-income countries, the domestic share remained relatively constant across decades.

The increase in domestic share in low- and middle-income countries was driven primarily by East Asia and Pacific (figure 2.8, panel b). Many countries in this region—including Indonesia, the Republic of Korea, Malaysia, the Philippines, Singapore, and Thailand—experienced financial crises during the late 1990s. After recovering, banks underwent restructurings, and financial regulation was strengthened. These countries focused on developing domestic debt markets to reduce the reliance on volatile international capital flows. This development of domestic bond markets is reflected in a rising share of domestic CNI—from 73 percent in 1990–99 to 84 percent in 2010–22.

The share of domestic issuance also grew significantly in South Asia—from 60 percent in 1990–99 to 80 percent in 2010–22. In low- and middle-income countries in other regions, the share of domestic market issuance has also risen since the 1990s, but firms continue to rely more on international capital. Latin America and the Caribbean, which ranks second in total CNI behind East Asia and Pacific, still exhibits considerable use of international capital markets, with about 40 percent of total CNI in international markets during 2010–22. Other regions rely similarly on international capital.

FIGURE 2.8

Domestic Market Shares of CNI Rose in Low- and Middle-Income Countries

a. By income group

Percent of CNI

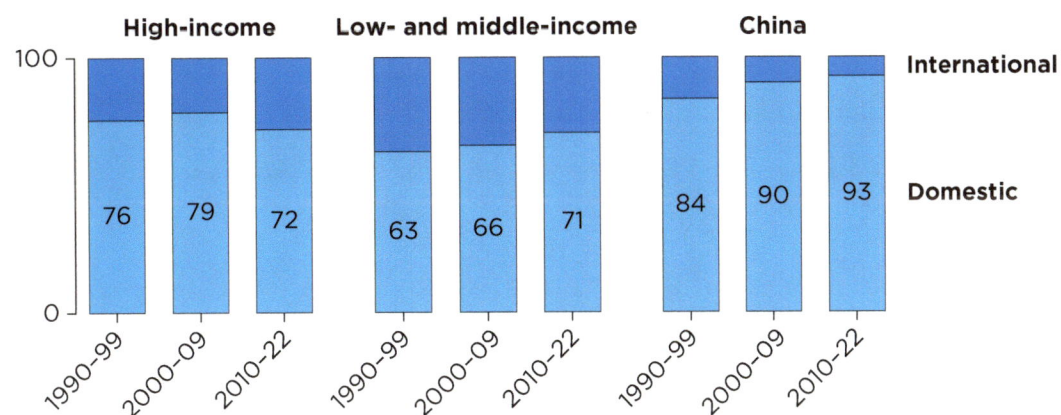

continued

FIGURE 2.8 *(Continued)*

b. By low- and middle-income regions

Percent of CNI

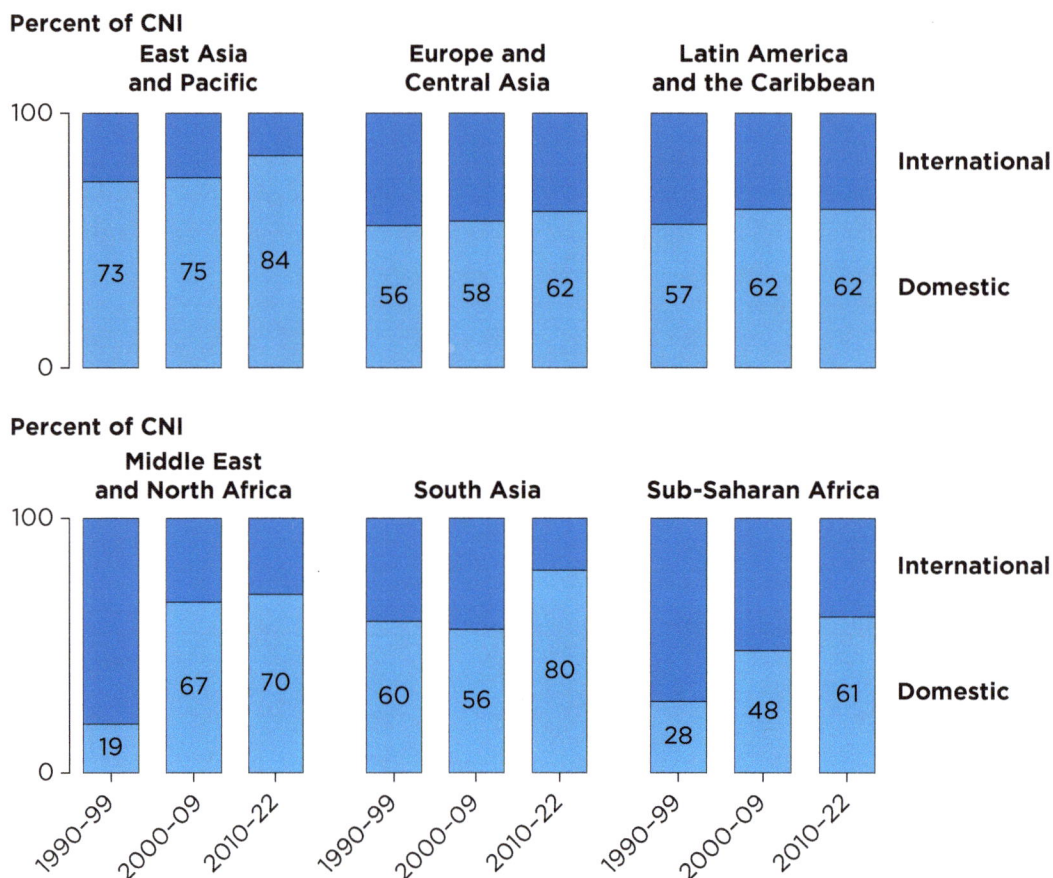

Percent of CNI

Source: Calculations using issuance data from the Securities Data Company Platinum database from LSEG.

Note: This figure presents the shares of CNI in domestic and international markets by income group and by region (for low- and middle-income countries only). CNI for year *Y* is computed as the sum of equity issuance and bond issuance (minus bonds that matured) between 1990 and year *Y*. The shares are calculated annually and then averaged across decades. Bonds are categorized as domestic or international by comparing the market location of issuance with the residence of the issuing firm. Equity is classified as domestic or international by comparing the location of the primary exchange where a firm's stock trades with the residence of the issuing firm. Appendix B provides the list of countries, grouped by income category. China is excluded from the East Asia and Pacific region. CNI = cumulative net capital issuance; GDP = gross domestic product.

Notes

1. The data refer to bond and stock values at issuance and hence are not influenced by subsequent capital gains, which would be reflected in secondary market prices.

2. Based on the World Bank country income classification, low- and middle-income countries are broken down into two subgroups: middle-income countries and low-income countries, excluding China. China is treated separately throughout the book given its economic ascent and size, which could otherwise distort the analysis for other country categories. The year for classifying countries into income groups is 1990 and is published by the World Bank (refer to appendix B). Although currently classified as a middle-income country, China was classified as a low-income country in 1990.

3. The book uses the period 1990 to 2022 to study long-run changes in capital market activity. In several exercises, it takes the 1990s as a base period and analyzes changes from the year 2000 onward, after the 1990s crises in low- and middle-income countries subsided and countries had implemented several capital market and macroeconomic reforms. The book also uses alternative periods to show the robustness of the results.

4. CNI as a ratio to GDP for year Y is computed as the sum of equity and bond issuance (minus bonds that matured) between 1990 and year Y, divided by GDP in year Y. When reported as decades, the figures are decade averages for such ratios.

5. In low- and middle-income countries, CNI increased from 0.1 percent of GDP in 1990 to 9 percent in 2000 and 18 percent in 2022.

6. Many countries, typically smaller countries with little participation in the global economy, have never tapped capital markets. Although developments in capital market access and use are associated with macroeconomic economic developments, the analysis in this book does not systematically relate the two.

7. Nine countries had only one issuance between 1990 and 2022: Micronesia in the 1990s, and Angola, Belarus, Kiribati, Libya, Madagascar, Maldives, Sudan, and Togo, thereafter.

8. In some countries, issuance may have abated or stopped owing to wars or other major disruptions.

9. As noted, the data used here do not capture instances in which equity is repurchased or retired.

10. Firms in middle-income countries experienced a boom in bond issuance in the 2000s, which was not witnessed in low-income countries (Abraham, Cortina, and Schmukler 2021).

11. Although this constraint is more significant for firms in low- and middle-income countries, it also applies, to a lesser extent, to firms in high-income countries. Appendix G provides details on the currency composition of issuance by firms from low- and middle-income countries across domestic and international markets.

12. Gozzi et al. (2015) show that a significant portion of firms continue to issue in domestic markets even after accessing international markets, suggesting that international markets are complements to rather than substitutes for domestic markets.

13. For firms in the euro area, bonds are classified as domestic or international based on the governing law under which they were issued. This approach is used because, after the adoption of the euro, firms in these countries began issuing most of their bonds in the eurobond market, even when the governing law was that of the firm's home country.

References

Abraham, F., J. J. Cortina, and S. L. Schmukler. 2021. "The Rise of Domestic Capital Markets for Corporate Financing: Lessons from East Asia." *Journal of Banking and Finance* 122 (January): 105987.

Gozzi, J. C., R. Levine, M. S. Martinez Peria, and S. L. Schmukler. 2015. "How Firms Use Corporate Bond Markets under Financial Globalization." *Journal of Banking & Finance* 58 (September): 532–51. https://doi.org/10.1016/j.jbankfin.2015.03.017.

Manconi, A., U. Peyer, and T. Vermaelen. 2019. "Are Buybacks Good for Long-Term Shareholder Value? Evidence from Buybacks around the World." *Journal of Financial and Quantitative Analysis* 54 (5): 1899–935.

CHAPTER 3

Expansion of Capital Markets across Firms

Pablo Hernando-Kaminsky

Key Messages

- The expansion of capital markets in low- and middle-income countries was mirrored by an influx of newly issuing firms.

- Since the late 1990s, the number of nonfinancial firms that raised capital annually in those markets increased fourfold in middle-income countries and fivefold in low-income countries, far surpassing the roughly 40 percent increase in high-income countries.

- As a result, a cohort of around 14,000 firms in low- and middle-income countries became new participants—firms that accessed capital markets for the first time between 2000 and 2022.

- These new participants have played a pivotal role in the growth of capital market financing for firms in low- and middle-income countries. By 2022, they accounted for the majority of cumulative net capital issuance (CNI) in low- and middle-income countries, a trend not mirrored in high-income countries.

- New participants were, on average, 21 years younger, had less than one-fifth of the assets, and issued less than half the amount of capital compared to "1990s participants"—firms that accessed capital markets at least once in the 1990s.

- Furthermore, both new and 1990s participants in low- and middle-income countries increasingly relied on domestic markets for their issuances. The average size of domestic bond issuances by first-time capital market participants was about 30 percent lower in 2010–22 than in 2000–09, suggesting improved access to domestic capital markets for smaller firms.

- The concentration of capital market activity—measured by the share of total issuance by each firm—declined in low- and middle-income countries due to the influx of new participants, although it remains higher than in high-income countries.

More Firms Are Raising Financing in Capital Markets

In addition to examining capital market growth across countries as in the previous chapter, it is also important to investigate how encompassing the expansion has been across firms within countries. The growth of capital markets in low- and middle-income countries has been accompanied by a rise in the number of firms tapping these markets. By 2022, these new participants accounted for the majority of CNI, unlike in high-income countries.

The number of nonfinancial firms issuing in a given year has risen in countries at all income levels, growing fivefold in low-income countries and fourfold in middle-income countries, but only 40 percent in high-income countries from the late 1990s to the peak in 2021 (figure 3.1).[1] This finding suggests that the expansion of capital markets may be attributed not solely to increased issuances from a few established firms but also to broader access for more firms.

FIGURE 3.1

More Firms Are Issuing Capital in All Income Groups

Number of issuing firms

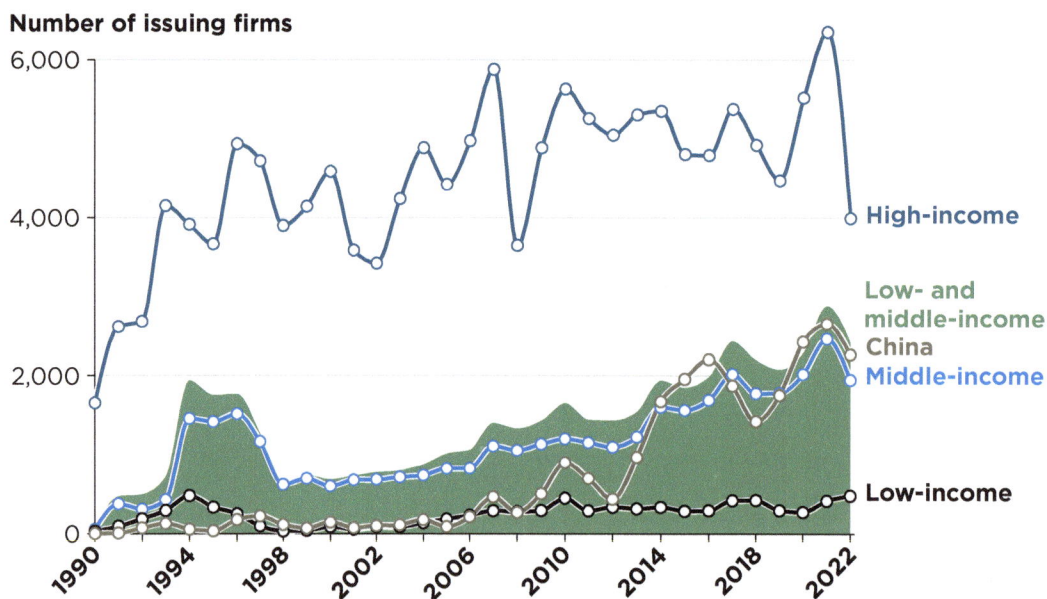

Source: Calculations using issuance data from the Securities Data Company Platinum database from LSEG.
Note: This figure presents the number of issuing firms in a given year for high-income countries and low- and middle-income countries (shaded area) as well as for subgroups within low- and middle-income countries and China. For each year, only the firms that issued equity or bonds during that year are counted. Appendix B provides the list of countries, grouped by income category.

The number of firms issuing annually rose to nearly 1,500 firms in middle-income countries and nearly 500 firms in low-income countries by the mid-1990s. The number fell in the late 1990–99 period before resuming growth after 2000. For China, the number of issuing firms remained broadly stable until 2010 and surged thereafter, reaching levels on par with the middle-income group of countries. During 1990–2022, about 20,000 firms in low- and middle-income countries participated in capital markets compared with 50,000 firms in high-income countries.

"1990s Participants" and "New Participants"

For this book's analysis, firms that issued stocks or bonds at some point during 1990–2022 are split into two groups: "1990s participants" refers to firms that issued in the 1990s (not necessarily exclusively), and "new participants" refers to firms that did not issue during the 1990s but did so subsequently (figure 3.2).[2] Firms are separated in this manner as a way of exploring the behavior of firms that had previously not tapped capital markets in the sample period, possibly because of constraints on their ability to do so, relative to the more established firms that were already active in capital markets in the 1990s.[3]

Among the total number of 20,000 firms in low- and middle-income countries and 50,000 firms in high-income countries that participated in capital markets between 1990 and 2022, approximately 6,000 firms in low- and middle-income countries and 21,000 firms in high-income countries are classified as "1990s participants." Meanwhile, 14,000 firms in low- and middle-income countries and 29,000 firms in high-income countries are classified as new participants between this period (table 3.1).[4]

As may be expected, new participants and 1990s participants differ significantly by age (measured as the number of years since a firm was founded), assets, and size of issuance during 2000–22 (table 3.2). On average, new participants are 21 years younger than 1990s participants. Firm size (proxied by assets held) and amounts issued are both larger for 1990s participants than for new participants.

FIGURE 3.2

Various Types of Firms Are Active in Capital Markets

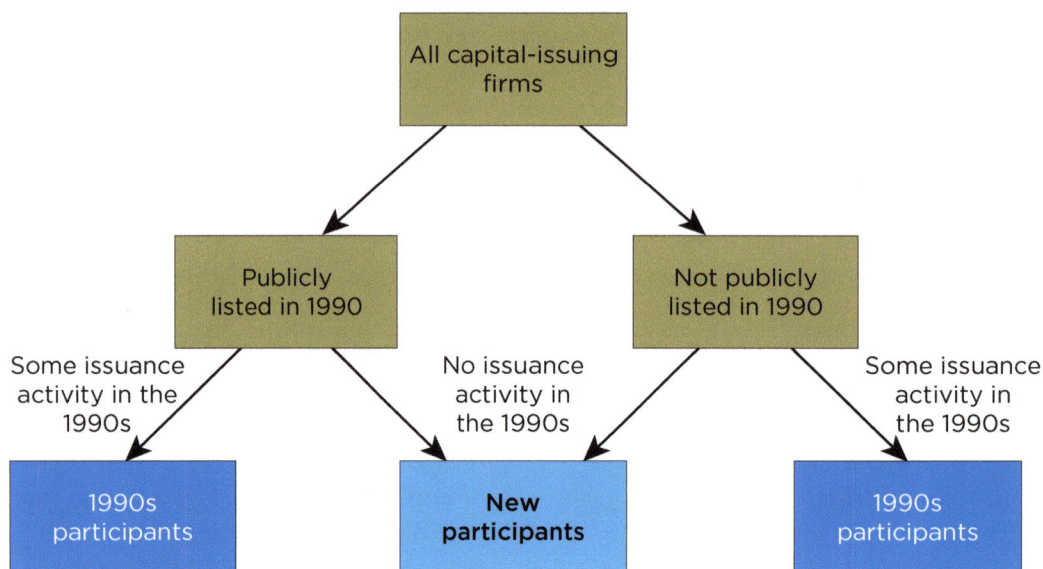

```
                        ┌─────────────────────┐
                        │ All capital-issuing  │
                        │        firms         │
                        └─────────────────────┘
                           ↙                ↘
           ┌─────────────────────┐    ┌─────────────────────┐
           │     Publicly        │    │    Not publicly     │
           │  listed in 1990     │    │   listed in 1990    │
           └─────────────────────┘    └─────────────────────┘
 Some issuance    ↙          ↘    No issuance  ↙       Some issuance
 activity in the          activity in            activity in
    1990s                 the 1990s               the 1990s
     ↓                        ↓                       ↓
┌──────────────┐      ┌──────────────┐      ┌──────────────┐
│   1990s      │      │    New       │      │   1990s      │
│ participants │      │ participants │      │ participants │
└──────────────┘      └──────────────┘      └──────────────┘
```

Sources: International Finance Corporation and World Bank.
Note: This figure presents the breakdown of capital-issuing firms based on whether they were publicly listed in 1990 and when they issued during 1990–2022.

TABLE 3.1

New Participants Constitute the Majority of Participants in Capital Markets, Regardless of Country Income Level

Type of participant	Low-income countries	Middle-income countries	China	High-income countries
1990s participants	1,684	4,324	802	20,881
New participants	3,645	10,722	8,982	28,994
Total	5,329	15,046	9,784	49,875

Source: Calculations using issuance data from the Securities Data Company Platinum database from LSEG.
Note: This table reports the number of 1990s and new participants for low-, middle-, and high-income countries, as well as China, during 1990–2022. Firms are considered 1990s participants if they issued at least once during the 1990s and new participants if they issued for the first time from 2000 onward.

TABLE 3.2

New Participants Were Younger and Smaller and Issued Smaller Amounts Than 1990s Participants during 2000–22

Characteristic	1990s Participants					New Participants				
	Number of firms	Mean	Median	P75	P90	Number of firms	Mean	Median	P75	P90
Age (years)	7,749	41	33	57	85	38,708	20	16	25	40
Assets (constant US$, millions)	9,159	16,854	2,438	13,582	42,702	34,984	2,978	73	543	4,084
Issuance (constant US$, millions)	10,545	361	117	363	837	53,885	141	24	132	342

Source: Calculations using issuance, assets, and age data from the Securities Data Company Platinum database from LSEG.
Note: This table presents several statistics for 1990s and new participants. Firms are considered 1990s participants if they issued at least once during the 1990s and new participants if they issued for the first time from 2000 onward. It reports descriptive statistics at the firm level for age, assets, and issuance. The first column provides the number of unique firms with nonmissing values for these characteristics in the Securities Data Company Platinum database. All the moments (the mean, median, 75th percentile [P75], and 90th percentile [P90] are computed using the pool of firms and years after 2000. Age is the number of years since a firm was founded. Assets and issuance are in millions of constant 2020 US dollars.

New Participants Account for a Large Share of Cumulative Net Capital Issuance in Low- and Middle-Income Countries

CNI in low-income countries, middle-income countries, and China experienced a significant uptick following the middle to late 2000s, increasing nearly threefold since then.[5] New participants contributed significantly to this expansion (figure 3.3). By 2022, CNI for new

FIGURE 3.3

New Participants Accounted for a Large Proportion of CNI in Low- and Middle-Income Countries

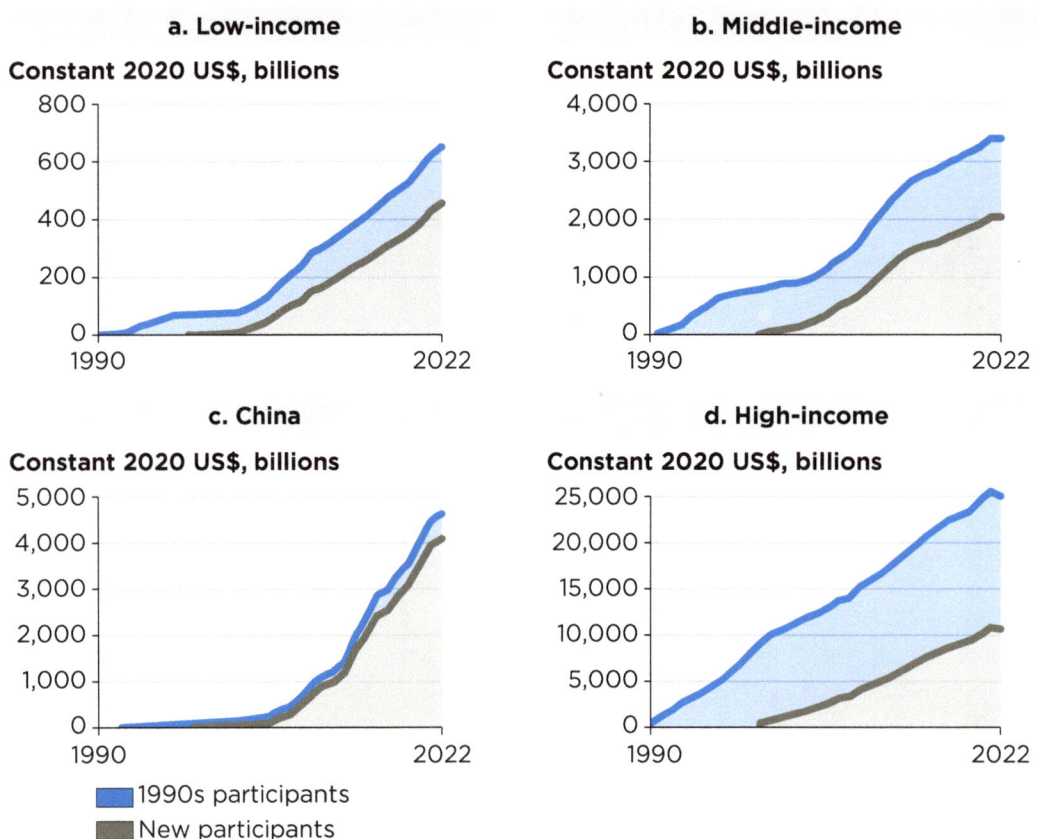

Source: Calculations using issuance data from the Securities Data Company Platinum database from LSEG.

Note: This figure shows the CNI for new and 1990s participants for the 1990–2022 period in billions of constant 2020 US dollars. CNI for year *Y* is computed as the sum of equity issuance and bond issuance (minus bonds that matured) between 1990 and year *Y*. Firms are considered 1990s participants if they issued at least once during the 1990s and new participants if they issued for the first time from 2000 onward. Appendix B provides the list of countries, grouped by income category. CNI = cumulative net capital issuance.

participants accounted for 61 percent of the total in low- and middle-income countries, with low- and middle-income countries at 70 percent and 60 percent, respectively—much higher than in high-income countries, where it was around 42 percent. In China, the share of new participants in CNI is particularly notable—at 88 percent by 2022.

Consistent with previous observations, there has been a significant increase in the share of CNI for new participants in low- and middle-income countries and China over time (figure 3.4, panel a). By 2010–22, the CNI for new participants in low- and middle-income countries had outgrown that of 1990s participants, while in China, CNI for new participants was almost six times that of 1990s participants. Although 1990s participants have always held the majority share in high-income countries, new participants' share has increased over time as well, growing from around 22 percent in 2000–09 to approximately 37 percent in 2010–22.

FIGURE 3.4

New Participants' Share of CNI Rose Substantially, Making Up the Majority of CNI across Most Regions in Low- and Middle-Income Countries

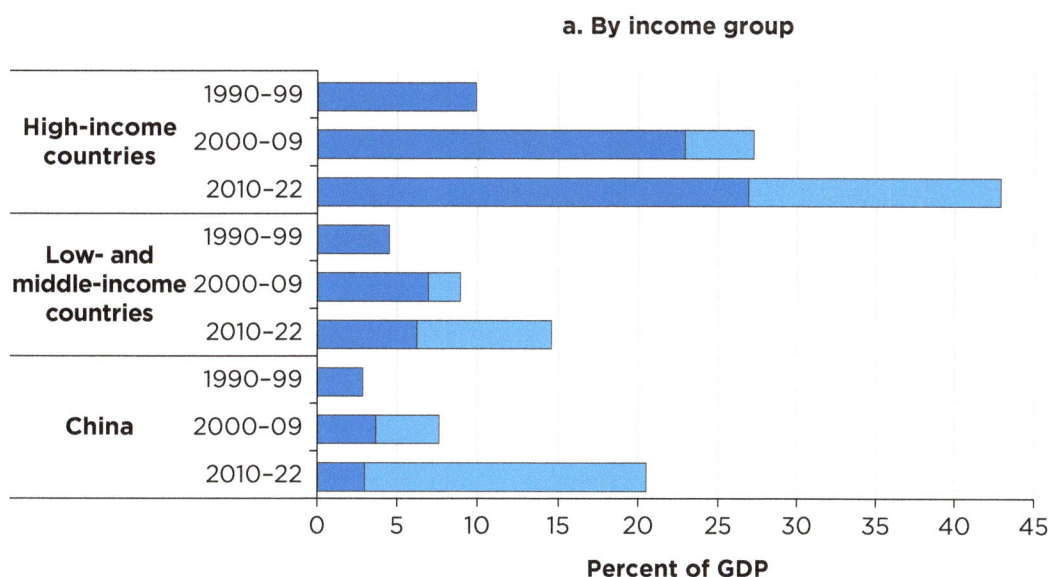

a. By income group

continued

FIGURE 3.4 *(Continued)*

b. By low- and middle-income region

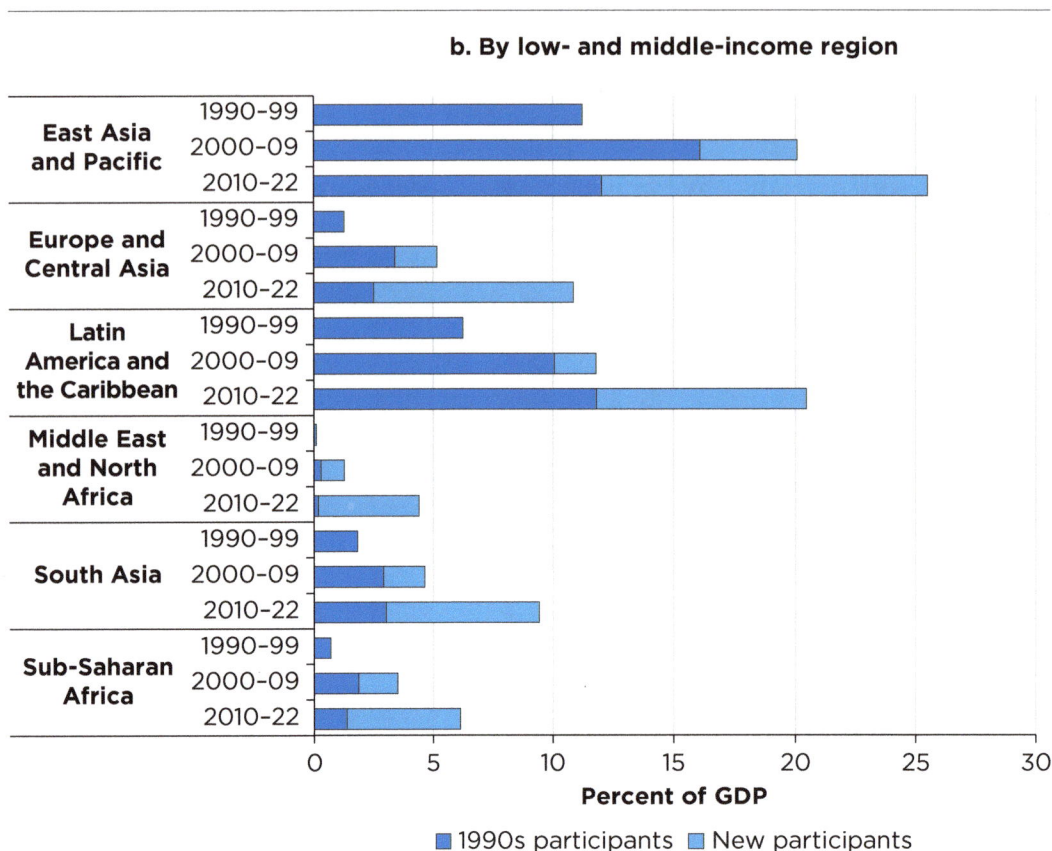

■ 1990s participants   ■ New participants

Sources: Calculations using issuance data from the Securities Data Company Platinum database from LSEG and GDP data from the World Bank's World Development Indicators.
Note: This figure shows the CNI (as a percentage of GDP) by new participants and 1990s participants by income group and by region (for low- and middle-income countries only). China is excluded from the East Asia and Pacific region (panel b). CNI as a ratio to GDP for year *Y* is computed as the sum of equity issuance and bond issuance (minus bonds that matured) between 1990 and year *Y*, divided by GDP in year *Y*. The figure reports decade averages for such ratios. Firms are considered 1990s participants if they issued at least once during the 1990s and new participants if they issued for the first time from 2000 onward. Appendix B provides the list of countries, grouped by income category. CNI = cumulative net capital issuance; GDP = gross domestic product.

The expansion of capital issuance by new participants is evident across all low- and middle-income regions (figure 3.4, panel b).[6] Particularly striking is the remarkable expansion of new participants in East Asia and Pacific. In 2010–22, their CNI surged, surpassing the issuance of 1990s participants.

In the Middle East and North Africa, where capital market activity was initially limited, new participants accounted for nearly all CNI during both 2000–09 and

2010–22. Similar patterns were observed in the remaining regions, with an increase in CNI for new participants and their share rising from 2000–09 to 2010–22.

Publicly Listed and Private New Participants Have Similar Characteristics

In the next chapter, the analysis compares new participants with 1990s participants, but owing to data limitations, this comparison is confined to publicly listed firms only. However, the following analysis shows that publicly listed new participants are similar to new participants that are not publicly listed, suggesting that the results in chapter 4 may apply to both types of firms.

As mentioned, the publicly listed status of a firm does not affect whether it is classified as a 1990s participant or a new participant. However, new participant firms that were publicly listed when they first issued between 2000 and 2022 have, by definition, previously issued equity (even if not observed in this sample).

The new participants that were publicly listed in the 1990s are an important cohort because, despite remaining inactive for several years, they have already paid the entry cost to be listed. These firms are crucial in the following chapter, which examines the effect of issuance on the aggregate stock of physical capital and employment.

With respect to age, amount of assets, and issuance size, new participants that were publicly listed in the 1990s are similar to new participants that were private in the 1990s and issued capital for the first time after the 1990s (table 3.3). The two groups account for a similar amount of capital raised after 2000.

In 2000–22, firms that were publicly listed in the 1990s were marginally older, averaging 22 years compared with 19 years for firms that were private during the same period. In terms of size, the two types of firms held nearly the same amount of assets on average. However, firms that were publicly listed in the 1990s issued slightly more capital (1.1 times). The values in table 3.3 are similar to those in table 3.2, where these two types of firms are aggregated, meaning that both groups of firms are much younger and smaller than 1990s participants.

Publicly listed and private new participants contribute comparably to total CNI in both middle-income and high-income countries (figure 3.5). In low-income countries, publicly listed new participants held the majority of CNI, accounting for approximately 46 percent of total CNI by 2022, while private new participants accounted for only 24 percent. The total includes values for 1990s participants. Conversely, in China, private new participants held the majority share, accounting for approximately 67 percent of total CNI by 2022, while publicly listed new participants accounted for only about 22 percent.

TABLE 3.3

Both Types of New Participants Were Similar with Regard to Age, Amount of Assets, and Issuance Size in 2000–22

Characteristic	Public in the 1990s					Private in the 1990s				
	Number of firms	Mean	Median	P75	P90	Number of firms	Mean	Median	P75	P90
Age (years)	14,571	22	16	29	49	24,137	19	15	23	35
Assets (constant US$, millions)	14,771	3,077	60	664	5,111	20,213	2,896	83	478	3,239
Issuance (constant US$, millions)	20,266	152	12	101	380	33,619	134	38	144	324

Source: Calculations using issuance, assets, and age data from the Securities Data Company Platinum database from LSEG.

Note: This table presents several statistics for new participants in 2000–22. Firms are considered new participants if they issued for the first time from 2000 onward. New participants are divided into firms that were publicly listed in the 1990s and those that were private in the 1990s. It reports descriptive statistics at the firm level for age, assets, and issuance. The first column provides the number of unique firms with nonmissing values for these characteristics in the database. All the moments (the mean, median, 75th percentile [P75], and 90th percentile [P90]) are computed using the pool of firms and years after 2000. Age is the number of years since a firm was founded. Assets and issuance are in millions of constant 2020 US dollars.

FIGURE 3.5

Publicly Listed and Private New Participants Accounted for Similar Shares of CNI in Countries at All Income Levels

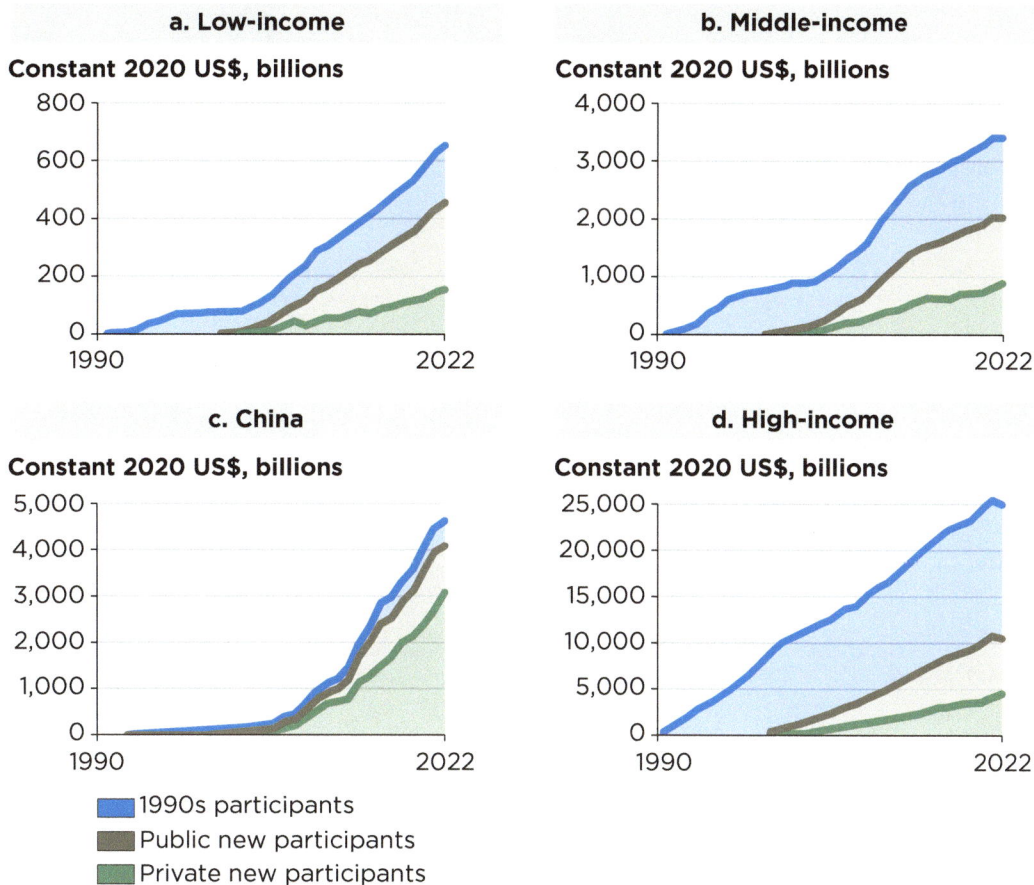

a. Low-income

Constant 2020 US$, billions

b. Middle-income

Constant 2020 US$, billions

c. China

Constant 2020 US$, billions

d. High-income

Constant 2020 US$, billions

- 1990s participants
- Public new participants
- Private new participants

Source: Calculations using issuance data from the Securities Data Company Platinum database from LSEG.

Note: This figure shows the CNI for new and 1990s participants for the 1990–2022 period in billions of constant 2020 US dollars. CNI for year *Y* is computed as the sum of equity issuance and bond issuance (minus bonds that matured) between 1990 and year *Y*. Firms are considered 1990s participants if they issued at least once during the 1990s and new participants if they issued for the first time from 2000 onward. New participants are divided into firms that were publicly listed in the 1990s and those that were private in the 1990s. Appendix B provides the list of countries, grouped by income category. CNI = cumulative net capital issuance.

Capital Market Concentration Declined in Low- and Middle-Income Countries

Market concentration across regions is assessed by constructing a normalized Herfindahl-Hirschman Index (HHI).[7] The HHI measures the size of gross capital issuance by firms relative to the size of total gross issuance of the country where they operate.[8] The HHI reflects the level of market concentration, with higher values indicating greater concentration. For instance, in a scenario where only one firm in a country issues capital, that firm would hold a 100 percent market share, resulting in an HHI of 1. As more firms tap capital markets, the HHI decreases.

Although the amount of CNI for new participants increased in low- and middle-income countries, China, and high-income countries, market concentration decreased in low- and middle-income countries and China, while remaining relatively stable in high-income countries over the past three decades (figure 3.6, panel a). The reduction has been significant in low- and middle-income countries, where market concentration dropped by about 31 percent, from 0.172 in 1990–99 to 0.118 in 2010–22. Despite this decline, market concentration of low- and middle-income countries has yet to reach the level of high-income countries. In China, market concentration fell below the level observed in high-income countries.

FIGURE 3.6

Market Concentration Declined in Low- and Middle-Income Countries between 1990 and 2022

a. By income group

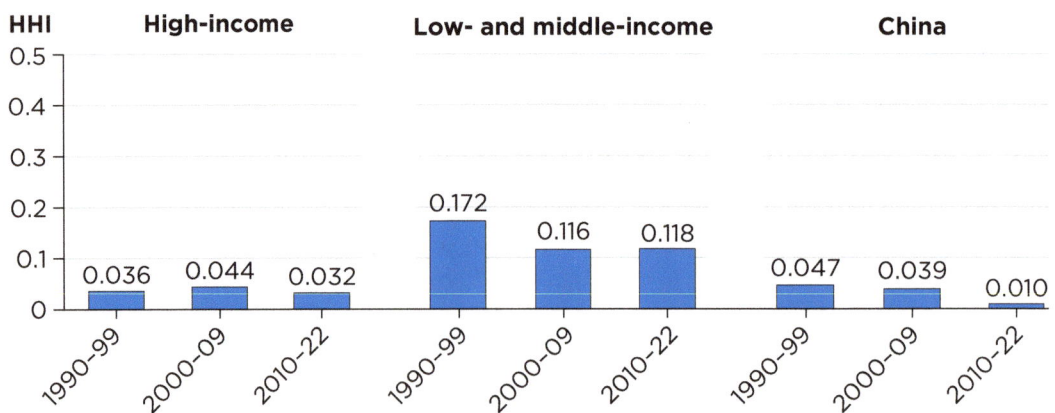

continued

FIGURE 3.6 *(Continued)*

b. By Low- and middle-income regions

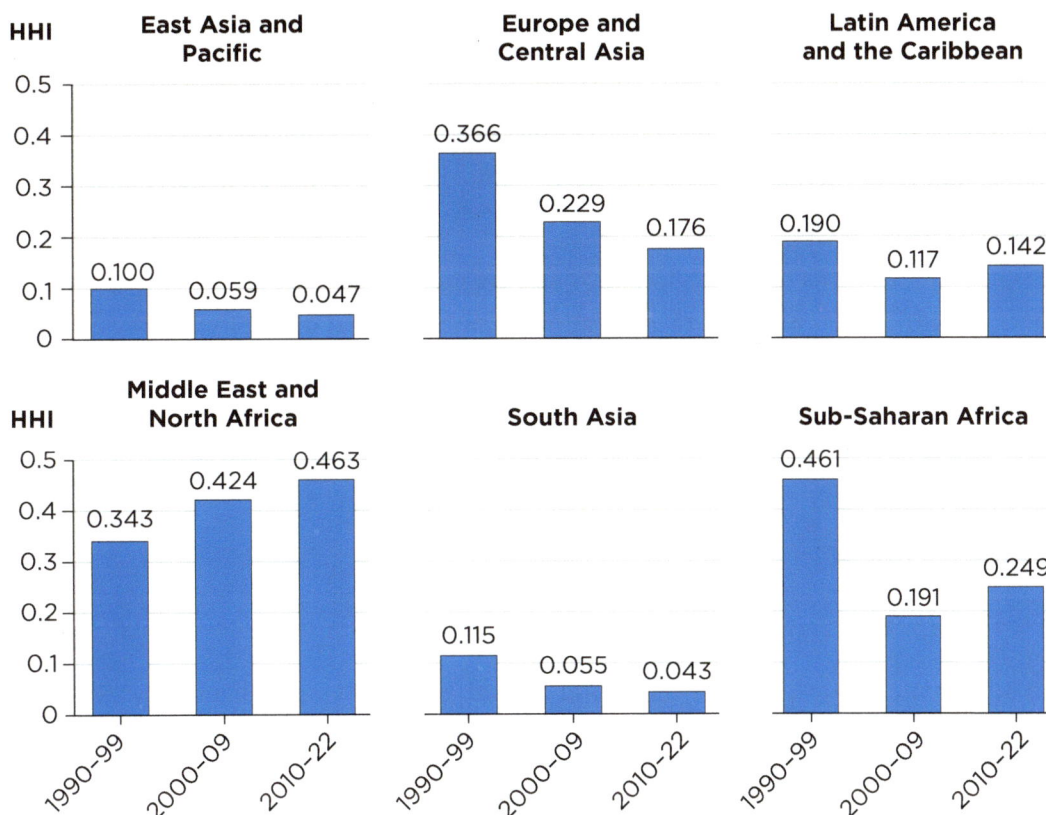

Source: Calculations using issuance data from the Securities Data Company Platinum database from LSEG.

Note: This figure presents the Herfindahl-Hirschman Index (HHI), first by income group and then by region (for low- and middle-income countries only). To calculate the HHI, a firm's share of total capital issued is calculated at the country-year level. Then, the HHI is calculated by squaring the market share of each issuing firm within a specific country and year, followed by the summation of these squared values. To obtain an income group or regional weighted average, the country index is weighted by the annual amount issued by a country in the overall group. Lastly, the average is calculated by decade. Appendix B provides the list of countries, grouped by income category. China is excluded from the East Asia and Pacific region.

Regions with initially larger capital markets, such as East Asia and Pacific and Latin America and the Caribbean, began with relatively small market concentrations in the 1990s (figure 3.6, panel b). As capital markets expanded in these regions over time, their market concentration declined even further. Europe and Central Asia and Sub-Saharan Africa, which started with smaller capital markets and have not yet reached the level of either East Asia and Pacific or Latin America and the Caribbean in 1990–99, also experienced a decline in their market concentration. In the Middle East and North Africa, despite the growth of capital markets over time and having the majority of new issuance in 2010–22 attributed to new participants, market concentration increased over time. This change occurred because, in many of the countries in the Middle East and North Africa, firms only entered capital markets after 2000. Even though firms in more countries were participating in capital markets, many of these previously nonissuing countries still only had a small number of firms issuing, leading to a higher average market concentration in the region.

Domestic Capital Markets Dominate for All Firms

In all income groups, most of the capital raised by both types of firms in 1990–2022 was issued in domestic markets (figure 3.7). In low- and middle-income countries, the average share of domestic CNI was 68 percent and 66 percent, respectively, for 1990s participants and 79 percent and 69 percent, respectively, for new participants in 1990–2022.[9] In China, the average share of domestic issuance for both types of firms was around 90 percent. In high-income countries, the average share of domestic issuance was 77 percent for 1990s participants and 67 percent for new participants in 1990–2022.

The crucial role of domestic capital markets in facilitating access for new participants in low- and middle-income countries warrants examining factors that can promote these markets. As the next chapter shows, such issuances also lead to significant aggregate economic outcomes, further motivating policy makers to develop domestic capital markets. Chapter 5 discusses potential drivers of growth of domestic capital markets in low- and middle-income countries.

FIGURE 3.7

Domestic Capital Markets Accounted for Most of CNI

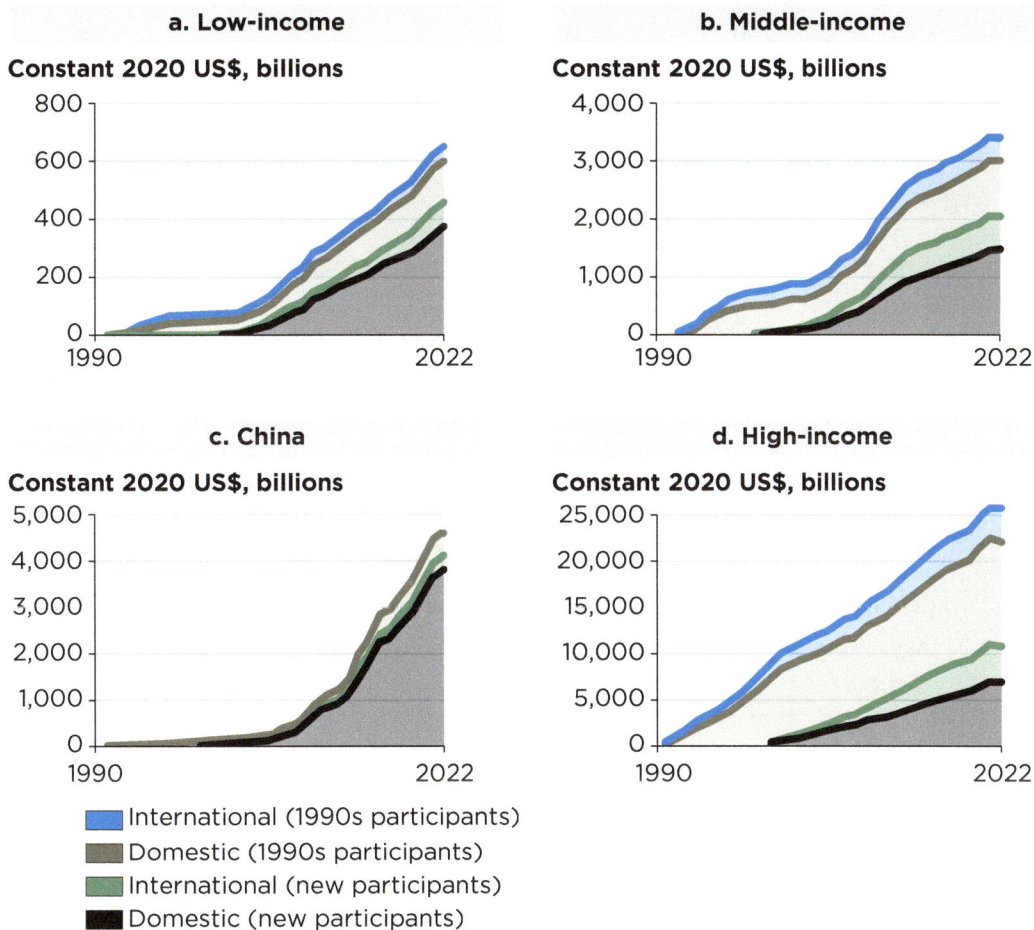

a. Low-income

Constant 2020 US$, billions

b. Middle-income

Constant 2020 US$, billions

c. China

Constant 2020 US$, billions

d. High-income

Constant 2020 US$, billions

■ International (1990s participants)
■ Domestic (1990s participants)
■ International (new participants)
■ Domestic (new participants)

Source: Calculations using issuance data from the Securities Data Company Platinum database from LSEG.
Note: This figure presents the amount of CNI for 1990s and new participants in domestic and international markets for 1990–2022 in billions of constant 2020 US dollars. CNI for year *Y* is computed as the sum of equity issuance and bond issuance (minus bonds that matured) between 1990 and year *Y*. Firms are considered 1990s participants if they issued at least once during the 1990s and new participants if they issued for the first time from 2000 onward. Bonds are categorized as domestic or international by comparing the market location of issuance with the residence of the issuing firm. Equity is classified as domestic or international by comparing the location of the primary exchange where a firm's stock trades with the residence of the issuing firm. Appendix B provides the list of countries, grouped by income category. CNI = cumulative net capital issuance.

Domestic Markets Are Important for First-Time Bond Issuers

Since bonds constitute the largest component of gross capital issuance, average bond size for first-time issuers across markets serves as an indicator of how new firms enter capital markets.[10] The average size of issuance can be used as a proxy for firm size.[11]

Across decades, international issuance has always been more sizable than domestic issuance. This is consistent with the view that larger firms, which have greater capacity to disclose information to foreign investors, are better able to access international capital markets. In addition, larger firms often require more capital to fund their projects. In international markets, the average amount issued by first-time bond issuers increased from US$473 million in 2000–09 to US$503 million in 2010–22. In contrast, the average amount issued in domestic markets has declined: first-time bond issuers issued, on average, US$211 million in 2000–09 and US$154 million in 2010–22, down about 30 percent (table 3.4). The findings suggest that smaller firms, which are typically younger, are gaining access to capital through domestic bond markets. Meanwhile, larger firms appear to issue their first bond in international markets. Notably, the decline in the size of domestic bond issuance drives an overall decline in the average size of first bond issuance, even after accounting for country dynamics.

TABLE 3.4

The Size of Domestic Bond Issuance Decreased, and the Size of International Bond Issuance Increased for First-Time Bond Issuers

| | 2000–09 | | |
	All Markets	**Domestic**	**International**
Mean	285.1	211.5	473.3
Std. Dev.	490.0	309.7	748.8
P25	60.9	45.1	156.0
P50	170.3	132.5	272.0
P75	320.3	260.7	506.5
P95	891.5	661.5	1,536.3

continued

TABLE 3.4 *(Continued)*

	2010–22		
	All Markets	**Domestic**	**International**
Mean	249.6	154.6	503.2
Std. Dev.	402.3	212.8	620.4
P25	58.5	49.1	182.9
P50	134.7	94.7	345.2
P75	292.7	175.9	589.1
P95	808.7	472.8	1,479.5

Source: Calculations using issuance data from the Securities Data Company Platinum database from LSEG.

Note: This table presents descriptive statistics for the amount issued for first-time bond issuers in domestic and international markets. The sample only includes firms that were not publicly listed on a stock exchange before issuing a bond and includes firms from all the countries. Bonds are categorized as domestic or international by comparing the market location of issuance with the residence of the issuing firm. The amount issued is in millions of constant 2020 US dollars. P25 = 25th percentile; P50 = 50th percentile (median); P75 = 75th percentile; P95 = 95th percentile; Std. Dev. = standard deviation.

Notes

1. For low- and middle-income countries, the number of nonfinancial firms issuing capital annually increased fourfold during the same period.

2. These criteria apply regardless of whether a firm was already publicly listed as of 1990. For instance, if a publicly listed firm did not issue any bonds or stocks during the 1990s, and did thereafter, it would be classified as a new participant. New participants may have issued prior to 1990 (before the start of the sample period). For the book's analyses, new participants refer to firms that only issued in the year 2000 onward during the 1990–2022 period.

3. The analysis is conducted by decades, with the 1990s chosen as the baseline decade. The results are robust to using other years as cutoffs for new participants. Appendix H presents the results using an alternate cutoff between the different groups (2010 instead of 2000).

4. On average, low- and middle-income countries have 194 firms per country (of which 57 are 1990s participants and 137 are new participants). High-income countries have 1,247 firms per country, on average (of which 522 are 1990s participants and 725 are new participants).

5. For low- and middle-income countries, capital increased in the mid-1990s. However, capital growth slowed by the end of the decade.

6. Expansion of capital issuance by new participants took place across all sectors (appendix I).

7. A normalized Herfindahl-Hirschman Index adjusts the standard HHI to a scale from 0 to 1 by accounting for the number of firms in a country in a particular year. This normalization standardizes the measure of market concentration, making it easier to compare across different income groups and regions.

8. The unnormalized Herfindahl-Hirschman Index (H) is calculated as $H = \sum_{i=1}^{N} s_i^2$, where s_i is the share of gross issuance by firm i in a given country, and N is the total number of issuing firms in that country. The normalized HHI is calculated as $HHI = \dfrac{(H - 1/N)}{1 - 1/N}$ *for* $N > 1$, and $HHI = 1$ *for* $N = 1$.

9. As appendix J shows, the domestic market share has been increasing in low- and middle-income countries over time.

10. Appendix F provides more details on gross capital issuances.

11. Data for firm-level assets are not well populated in the Securities Data Company Platinum database. Therefore, issuance is used as a proxy for size (Gozzi et al. 2015).

Reference

Gozzi, J. C., R. Levine, M. S. Martinez Peria, and S. L. Schmukler. 2015. "How Firms Use Corporate Bond Markets under Financial Globalization." *Journal of Banking and Finance* 58 (September): 532–51. https://doi.org/10.1016/j.jbankfin.2015.03.017.

CHAPTER 4

Economic Outcomes of Issuing Capital

Manuel García-Santana

Key Messages

- Issuing in capital markets was followed by a rise in firms' physical capital, employment, and sales, suggesting that firms use productively the capital raised through bond or stock issuance. This association was stronger for new participants (firms that accessed capital markets only from 2000 onward) and firms issuing equity.

- Before their participation in capital markets, new participants were younger and smaller (with regard to sales, physical capital, and employment) than 1990s participants. Especially in low- and middle-income countries, they also exhibited a higher marginal return to capital (MRK)—defined as the additional output a company would generate from using an extra unit of capital.

- After new participants raised funds in capital markets, they experienced a decline in their MRK, suggesting that capital markets activity helped these firms relax their financial constraints.

- Because firms with a higher MRK raised more funds (that is, more capital went to the firms where it would have a bigger bang for the buck), capital markets generated a more efficient allocation of capital across firms. When more capital goes to the firms that generate the most output per unit of capital, economywide total output increases.

- These patterns are stronger for low-income countries than for middle-income countries.

As shown in the preceding chapters, a feature of capital market growth in low-and middle-income countries was the expanding role of new participants (firms that accessed capital markets only after 2000), with these firms accounting for a rising share of issuances globally over 2000–22. Additionally, new participants were younger and smaller, on average, than 1990s participants (firms that issued in the 1990s). Given the substantial amount of financing being directed to new participants, this chapter investigates the potential effects of their participation on economic outcomes.

The analysis in this chapter focuses on two channels through which capital markets can affect economic outcomes. First, participating in capital markets can provide firms with additional financing to employ more capital and labor—that is, to increase the amount of production factors they use. Second, capital markets can help to improve efficiency in the economy if the firms with an expanding role are precisely the ones with a relatively high MRK.

Two critical aspects are considered to investigate these channels. First, it is necessary to determine whether new participants used the funds to raise their production, for example, by increasing their stock of capital, or to change their capital structure, for example, by repurchasing existing equity. The answer determines whether increased participation in capital markets results in stronger use of production factors.

Second, it is important to determine whether new participants exhibited higher MRK before participating in capital markets, compared with 1990s participants. If so, this characteristic would be consistent, for instance, with new participants facing higher financial constraints before they gained access to capital markets. In that case, it is likely that increased financing for new participants would improve economic outcomes.

Properly measuring firms' characteristics, such as their MRK, and analyzing the real effects of firm issuances in capital markets require data from firms' income statements and balance sheets. Because such data are only available in the data used in this book for publicly listed firms (a subset of firms issuing in capital markets), the analysis in this chapter focuses on that group of firms.[1] As publicly listed firms are more mature, larger, and more capital-intensive than the vast majority of firms, the sample of firms in this chapter is not representative of the whole population of firms, especially for low- and middle-income countries. The results will show that even though these firms are well established in their industries, their performance improves after issuance episodes.

Within publicly listed firms, the analysis distinguishes between two groups: 1990s participants and new participants. As in previous chapters, firms are 1990s participants if they issued at least one security in the 1990s and new participants if they had no issuance activity during the 1990s but issued subsequently. As shown in chapter 3, publicly listed new participants are similar to private new participants in age, total assets, and size of issuances at the time of issuance during the 2000–22 period. In addition, they accounted for about half of the capital market activity of all new participants.

The first section of this chapter provides evidence on the main attributes of new participants. It compares new participants with 1990s participants, measuring firm characteristics in the 1990s—that is, before new participants experienced any capital market activity. The second section analyzes the real effects of participating in capital markets for firms, quantifying their economic performance before and after issuance. The third section studies the impact of capital market financing on aggregate economic outcomes, differentiating between new and 1990s participants.

What Are the Characteristics of New Participants before They Participated in Capital Markets?

For the sample of publicly listed firms, the characteristics of new participants are compared with those of 1990s participants operating in the same industry—defined at the two-digit Standard Industrial Classification (SIC)—and country. For example, new and 1990s participants are compared in the transport equipment industry in Brazil in the same years.[2]

The analysis focuses on size, age, and MRK. Box 4.1 (and appendix K in more detail) explains how these variables are measured in the data. Size and age are often considered important predictors of firms' ability to create employment and innovate and the extent to which firms may be financially constrained (Cohen 2010; Ferreira, Haber, and Rorig 2023; Gertler and Gilchrist 1994). MRK captures the additional output a firm would produce if an additional unit of capital was allocated to it. The motivation for studying new participants' MRK is to measure the extent to which increasing financing by these firms in capital markets can generate a better allocation of capital across firms and thus better aggregate economic outcomes.

BOX 4.1

Measuring Firm Characteristics

The variables measuring a firm's age, size, and marginal return to capital (MRK) are computed as follows:

- Size is measured using information available in the firm's balance sheet and income statement. Throughout the chapter, the analysis focuses on three measures: physical capital (measured by property, plant, and equipment), sales (measured by net sales), and employment (measured by number of employees). Because the balance sheet and income statement data used in this book only covers publicly listed firms, most firms in the sample are large relative to all firms operating in low- and middle-income countries. For example, the median firm in the data set has sales and physical capital of around US$58 million and US$17 million, respectively, and employs around 404 employees (see appendix K for details).

- Age refers to the number of years since the firm's foundation.

- MRK is not observed because it refers to the marginal value a company would generate from an additional unit of capital. Under standard assumptions regarding consumers' demand and firms' technology, MRK can be calculated as the average return to capital multiplied by the output elasticity of capital. Under the assumption that this elasticity is the same for firms producing in the same industry and country (and remains constant over time), production function estimation techniques can be applied to estimate it. The analysis here follows the approach taken in most studies, which is to compute a firm's MRK as the product of its average return to capital (computed by dividing the firm's revenue by its physical capital) and an industry-level output elasticity of capital.[a]

a. The industry-level output elasticities are estimated following Levinsohn and Petrin (2003). Appendix L offers details.

Understanding why firms exhibit a high or a low MRK has been central in studies investigating the causes and consequences of misallocation of resources across firms in low- and middle-income countries. One reason why dispersion in MRK can exist is related to the fact that adjusting their capital stock to business opportunities may be too costly for some firms (Asker, Collard-Wexler, and de Loecker 2014). Another reason is related to the amount of information that firms have when deciding how much capital to add (David, Hopenhayn, and Venkateswaran 2016). For example, they may not have adequate information about future business opportunities. Differences in risk across firms may also explain dispersion in MRK (David, Schmid, and Zeke 2022; appendix M offers a detailed discussion).

Perhaps the most common interpretation of dispersion in firm MRK is that different firms may have differential access to financing (for example, Gopinath et al. 2017). If a firm exhibits a relatively high MRK, the potential gain from using additional capital is large. The fact that the firm has a high MRK reflects its inability to obtain capital, indicating that it is financially constrained. Otherwise, the firm would expand to exploit its business opportunities.

Considering firms producing in the same country and industry, new participants in low- and middle-income countries were smaller, younger, and exhibited a higher MRK than 1990s participants. These differences are bigger when comparing new participants with highly active 1990s participants (determined by the number of issuances in the 1990s). Differences in the MRK are larger in low-income countries than in middle-income countries and are significantly smaller in high-income countries. These results are shown in table 4.1, which reports the percentiles where new participants and 1990s participants were located in their respective industry-country distributions of age, physical capital, employment, sales, and MRK.[3]

What Are the Real Effects of Firms' Issuing Activity?

Access to capital markets does not necessarily imply real effects on firms' performance. For example, firms might substitute bank credit with the newly available source of financing in capital markets. Under that scenario, participation in capital markets would change firms' debt structure but not affect their performance.

TABLE 4.1

New Participants Were Younger and Smaller and Exhibited a Higher MRK Than 1990s Participants

Income group	Firm type	Age	Physical capital	Employment	Sales	MRK
LICs	New participants	44.6	49.9	49.1	48.3	46.7
	1990s participants	61.7	62.2	58.5	55.2	37.7
	Top 25% 1990s participants	67.5	84.1	65.4	80.5	27.8
	Top 10% 1990s participants	69.9	87.0	79.9	84.8	27.0
MICs	New participants	46.3	48.8	48.7	48.7	51.9
	1990s participants	58.7	53.1	52.7	53.9	48.7
	Top 25% 1990s participants	63.0	64.6	61.6	64.7	44.8
	Top 10% 1990s participants	65.0	77.7	69.5	73.6	42.8
China	New participants	46.0	33.4	39.9	42.3	58.4
	1990s participants	76.4	59.1	52.2	54.4	45.5
	Top 25% 1990s participants	79.0	81.4	59.4	75.3	42.6
	Top 10% 1990s participants	70.7	89.6	67.8	87.0	42.4
HICs	New participants	43.9	38.0	42.2	37.8	50.5
	1990s participants	65.2	55.4	56.5	54.2	50.4
	Top 25% 1990s participants	72.9	78.2	76.9	76.0	41.7
	Top 10% 1990s participants	77.9	85.6	83.7	84.4	38.7

Sources: Calculations using issuance data from the Securities Data Company Platinum database and firm balance sheet data from Worldscope, both from LSEG. Appendix K provides details.

Note: The table reports the percentile of the average new participant, the average 1990s participant, and the top 25 percent and top 10 percent most active 1990s participants (measured by the number of issuances in the 1990s) in their respective industry-country distribution of age, physical capital, employment, sales, and MRK. These percentiles are based on the standardized firms' characteristics measured in the 1990s. Industries are classified according to Standard Industrial Classification two-digit codes. Firms are considered 1990s participants if they issued at least once during the 1990s and new participants if they issued for the first time from 2000 onward. The number of new participants and 1990s participants is 2,597 and 1,095, respectively, in low-income countries; 4,997 and 2,727 in middle-income countries; 3,837 and 704 in China; and 21,257 and 17,355 in high-income countries. Appendix B provides the list of countries, grouped by income category. HICs = high-income countries; LICs = low-income countries: MICs = middle-income countries; MRK = marginal return to capital.

Another way to think about the real effects of capital market participation is linked to whether the firm is financially constrained or not at the time of the issuance. If the firm is financially constrained, extra funds obtained in capital markets will likely be used for productive purposes. For example, activity in capital markets would be associated with a rise in firms' physical capital and employment, eventually increasing sales.

One should also expect a larger effect on physical capital than on employment since financial constraints are more likely to affect inputs requiring larger up-front investments. For example, firms might need to raise large sums to purchase new machinery, especially for indivisible investments, but those funds might not be needed to hire employees. Still, to the extent that machinery and labor are complements, both of them could react to capital-raising activity in some instances.

The analysis compares the evolution of sales, employment, physical capital, and MRK of a firm issuing in capital markets with other firms operating in the same industry and country. To that end, local projection regressions are estimated (Jordà 2005). In particular, the cumulative difference of a specific variable (physical capital, sales, employment, or MRK) is regressed against a dummy variable that takes the value 1 if the firm issues in a specific year (and zero otherwise) alongside several controls, including firm, year-industry, and year-country fixed effects. The effect is identified by comparing the change in trajectory of a firm that issues in a given period with the change in trajectory of a firm (from the same industry and country) that does not.

To analyze the dynamic effect of issuance activity, the cumulative difference of the variables is computed at different time horizons. Caution must be taken when interpreting the reported estimates as causal. For example, firms may endogenously choose to participate in capital markets after finding a good business opportunity.

Issuance activity is associated with an increase in sales, physical capital, and employment. One year after the issuance ($t = 1$), the increase is 11 percent for sales, 17 percent for physical capital, and 8 percent for employment. A sizable portion of these effects remains positive (statistically different from zero at the customary levels of significance) after four years (figure 4.1).

The results in figure 4.1 are from estimations that pool all countries together. The estimated effects on physical capital and sales are qualitatively similar when focusing separately on middle-income countries and low-income countries (figure 4.2), with stronger and longer-lasting effects for the case of low-income countries. For instance, one year after the issuance, the increase in sales and physical capital is 10 percent and 15 percent, respectively, for firms in low-income countries, compared with 4 percent and 8 percent, respectively, for firms in middle-income countries (figure 4.2). In the case of employment, an effect of 5 percent is estimated one year after the issuance for firms in low-income countries, whereas it is close to zero for firms in middle-income countries.

FIGURE 4.1

Issuance Activity Is Followed by an Increase in Sales, Physical Capital, and Employment

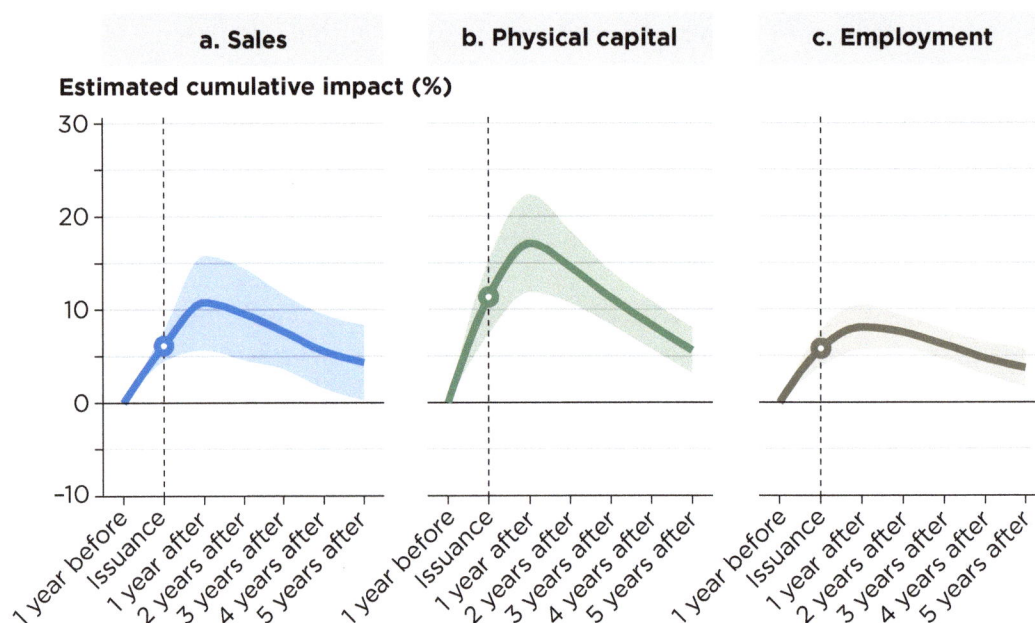

Sources: Calculations using issuance data from the Securities Data Company Platinum database and firm balance sheet data from Worldscope, both from LSEG. Appendix K provides details.

Note: This figure shows the estimated cumulative impact (in percentages) of a firm's issuance in the year of issuance ($t = 0$) and in the following five years as well as its 95 percent confidence intervals for sales, physical capital, and employment. The baseline for estimating cumulative impact is the year before issuance. These regressions include all countries in the sample (appendix B provides a complete list of countries). The number of firms used in these regressions (averaged across the time horizons) is 58,566 for physical capital, 56,700 for sales, and 42,307 for employment.

FIGURE 4.2

Firms' Real Effects of Issuance Activity Are Stronger in
Lower-Income Countries Than in Middle-Income Countries

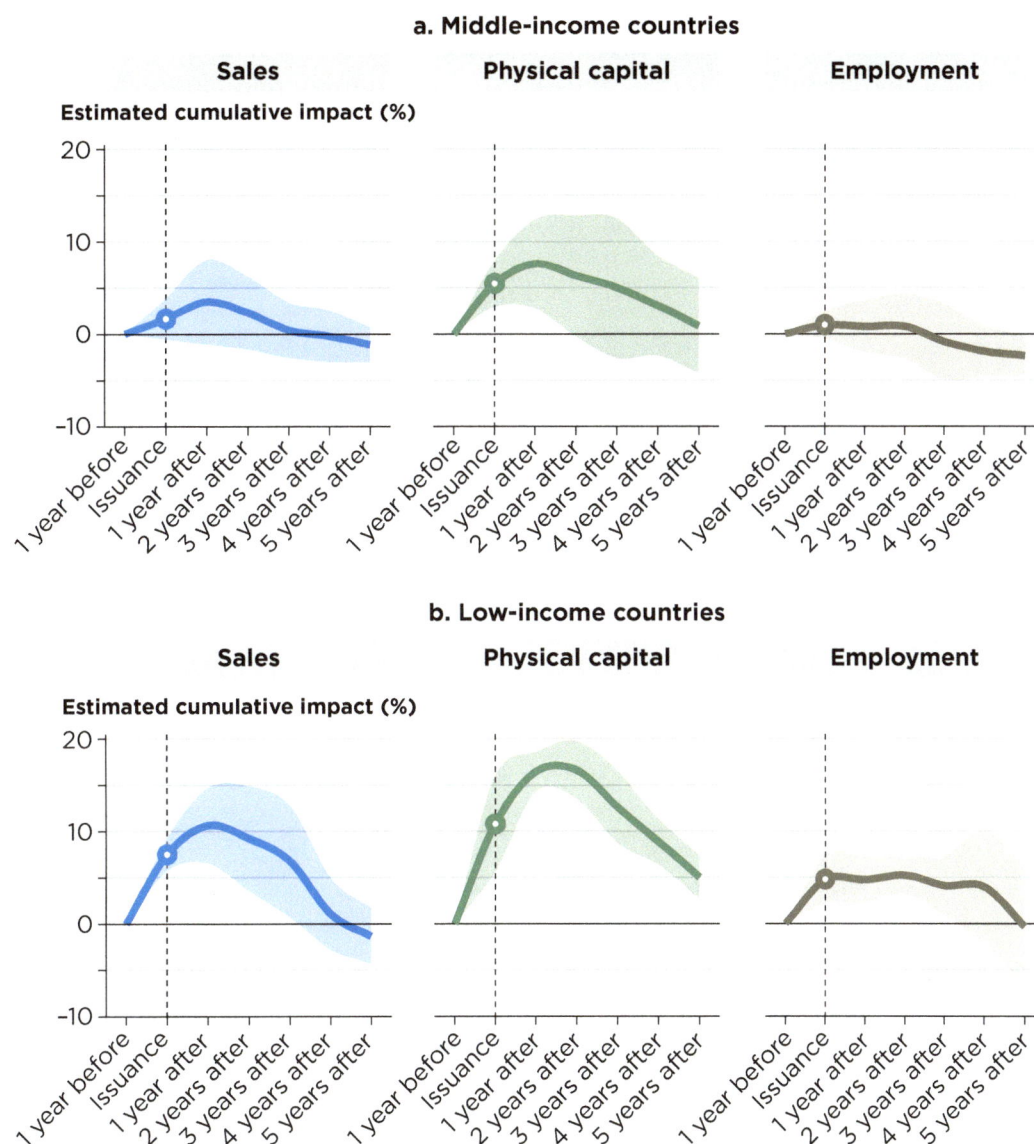

a. Middle-income countries

Sales Physical capital Employment

Estimated cumulative impact (%)

b. Low-income countries

Sales Physical capital Employment

Estimated cumulative impact (%)

Sources: Calculations using issuance data from the Securities Data Company Platinum
database and firm balance sheet data from Worldscope, both from LSEG. Appendix K
provides details.

Note: This figure shows the estimated cumulative impact (in percentages) of a firm's
issuance in the year of issuance ($t = 0$) and in the following five years as well as its
95 percent confidence intervals for sales, physical capital, and employment. The baseline
for estimating cumulative impact is the year before issuance. These effects are presented
for middle-income countries and low-income countries. Appendix B provides the list of
countries, grouped by income category. The number of firms used in these regressions
(averaged across the time horizons) is 10,341 for physical capital, 10,341 for sales, and 6,169
for employment in the case of middle-income countries and 5,772 for physical capital,
5,758 for sales, and 2,442 for employment in the case of low-income countries.

The effects are stronger for new participants. For these firms, the increase after one year ($t = 1$) is about 10 percent for sales, 18 percent for physical capital, and 8 percent for employment. These numbers compare to 6 percent, 6 percent, and 3 percent, respectively, for the top 10 percent most active 1990s participants (with regard to issuances in 1990s). Additionally, a higher portion of these effects persists after four years for new participants (figure 4.3). New participants in low- and middle-income countries also exhibit stronger effects (unreported results).[4]

The effects are stronger for new participants despite the smaller size of their issuances. The mean equity issuance had a value of US$128 million for new participants, compared with US$270 million for the top 10 percent of 1990s participants. For bonds, the average issuance by new participants was US$88 million, one-tenth the size of issuance by 1990s participants, US$852 million.

These impacts are particularly strong for the first issuance. The effect after one year was 11 percent for sales, 28 percent for physical capital, and 12 percent for employment for the first issuance, compared with 10 percent, 12 percent, and 6 percent, respectively, for subsequent issuances. Moreover, these effects for subsequent issuances tend to disappear faster (unreported results).

FIGURE 4.3

Firms' Real Effects of Issuance Activity Are Stronger for New Participants Than for 1990s Participants

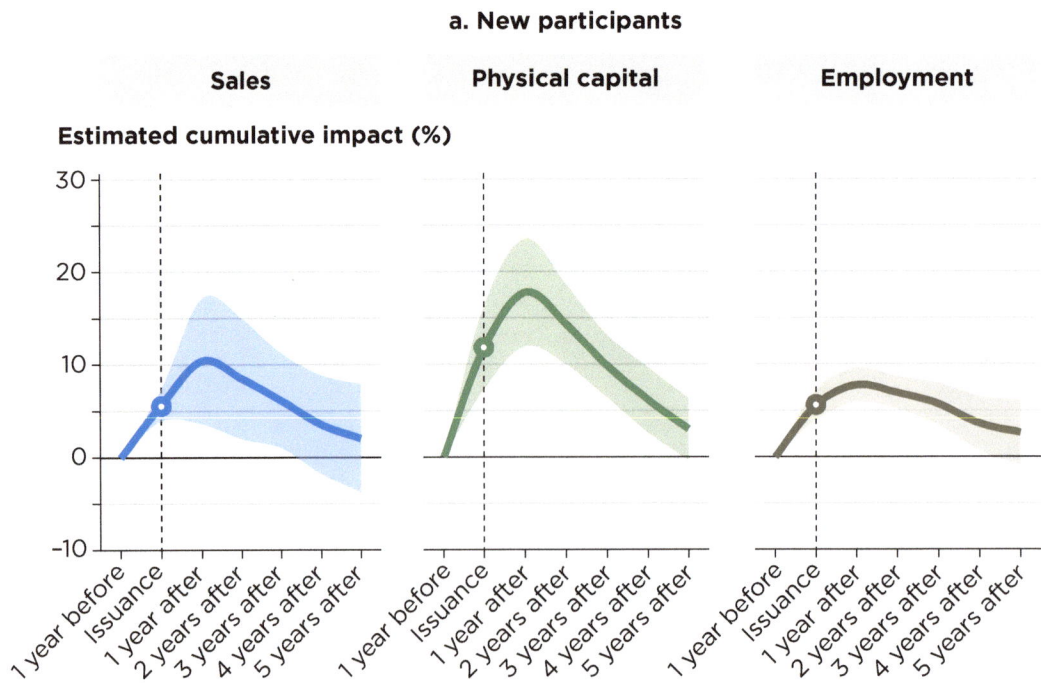

a. New participants

Estimated cumulative impact (%)

continued

continued

FIGURE 4.3 *(Continued)*

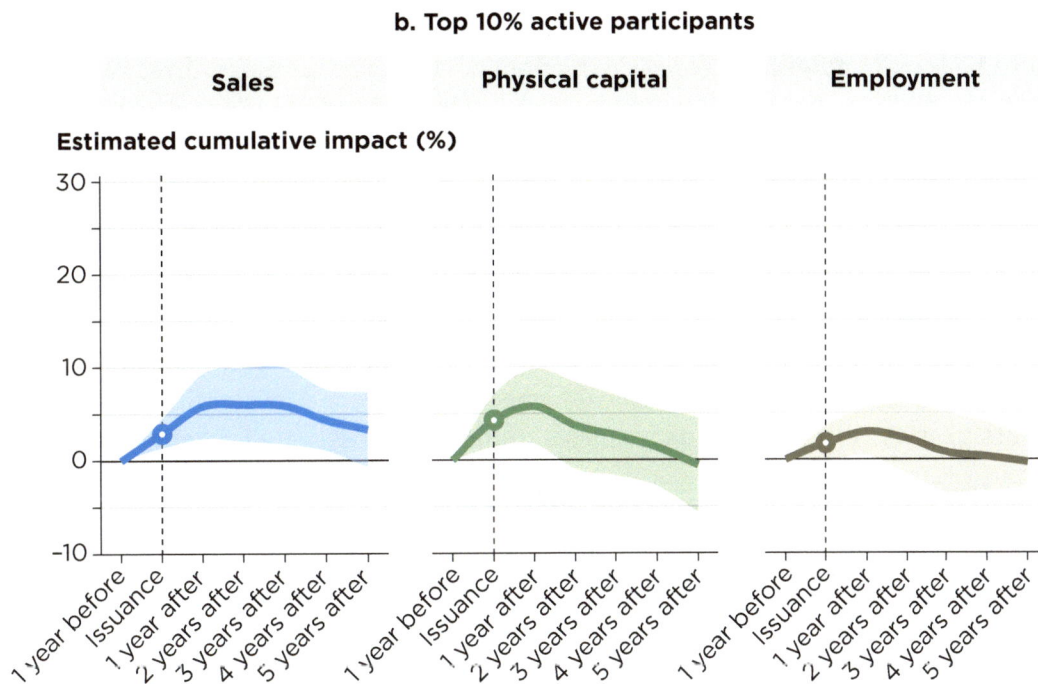

b. Top 10% active participants

Sales   Physical capital   Employment

Sources: Calculations using issuance data from the Securities Data Company Platinum database and firm balance sheet data from Worldscope, both from LSEG. Appendix K provides details.

Note: This figure shows the estimated cumulative impact (in percentages) of a firm's issuance in the year of issuance ($t = 0$) and in the following five years as well as its 95 percent confidence intervals for sales, physical capital, and employment. The baseline for estimating cumulative impact is the year before issuance. Firms are considered 1990s participants if they issued at least once during the 1990s and new participants if they issued for the first time from 2000 onward. The regressions include all countries in the sample. Appendix B provides a complete list of countries. The number of firms used in these regressions (averaged across the time horizons) is 43,193 for physical capital, 41,452 for sales, and 28,759 for employment in the case of new participants and 1,253 for physical capital, 1,250 for sales, and 1,170 for employment in the case of the top 10 percent most active 1990s participants.

Why could issuing in capital markets be particularly relevant for a firm that has not engaged in such activity for many years? One potential explanation is that firms use the first issuances to pursue their most profitable activities, which would also be consistent with a stronger reduction in MRK. Furthermore, firms issuing bonds could use subsequent issuances to roll over maturing bonds, with less significant effects on their productive activity.

What Are the Effects of Issuance Activity on Firms' Marginal Return to Capital?

High MRK is often interpreted as signaling that a firm is financially constrained. As shown, new participants exhibited higher MRK before participating in capital markets in the 2000s. But what happens to the firm's MRK after issuance?

Issuance is followed by a reduction in MRK. The impact after a year is estimated at around 5 percent. A portion of this reduction persists three years after the issuance. The reduction is driven by firms increasing their stock of physical capital, consistent with a relaxation of financial constraints.

The reduction in MRK holds only for new participants. Whereas the effect is 6 percent after one year for new participants, its counterpart for the top 10 percent of 1990s participants is close to zero over all time horizons and is not statistically significant. This result is consistent with new participants being financially constrained before participating in capital markets, unlike the top 10 percent of 1990s participants, and relaxing that constraint ex post (figure 4.4). A similar pattern is found when focusing on new participants operating in low- and middle-income countries (unreported results).

The reduction in MRK one year after the issuance episode is slightly stronger for firms operating in low-income countries, about 6 percent, than it is for firms operating in middle-income countries, about 4 percent. The effects on MRK also persist longer in low-income than in middle-income countries (figure 4.5).

FIGURE 4.4

Issuance Activity Is Associated with a Reduction in Firms' MRK

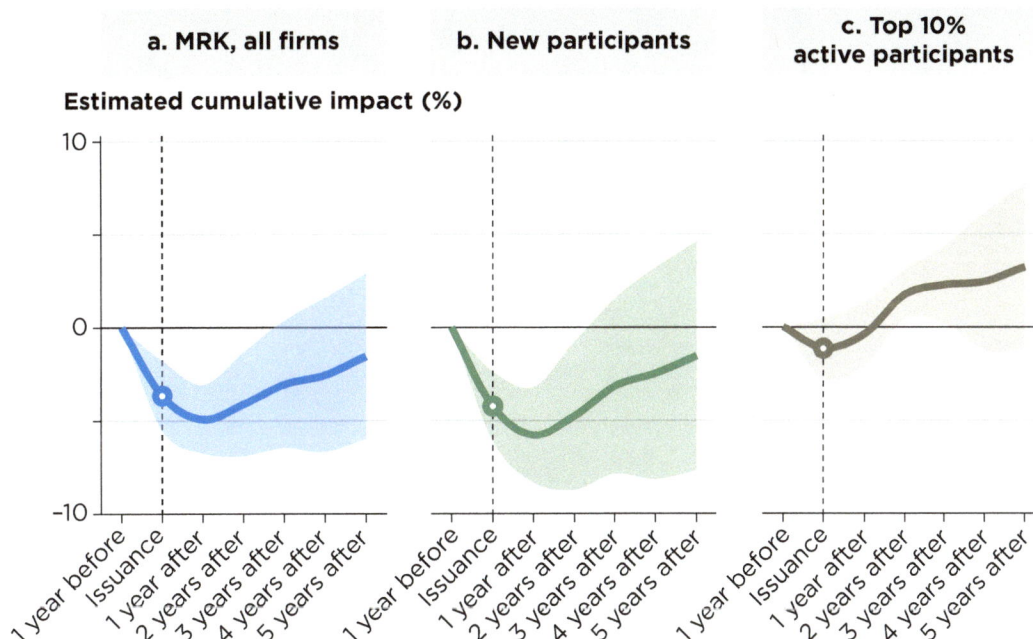

a. MRK, all firms   **b. New participants**   **c. Top 10% active participants**

Estimated cumulative impact (%)

Sources: Calculations using issuance data from the Securities Data Company Platinum database and firm balance sheet data from Worldscope, both from LSEG. Appendix K provides details.

Note: This figure shows the estimated cumulative impact (in percentages) of a firm's issuance in the year of issuance ($t = 0$) and in the following five years as well as its 95 percent confidence intervals for MRK. Panel a shows the results for all firms together. Panel b shows the results for new participants. Panel c shows the results for the top 10 percent most active 1990s participants (measured as the number of issuances in the 1990s). The baseline for estimating cumulative impact is the year before issuance. Firms are considered 1990s participants if they issued at least once during the 1990s; they are considered new participants if they issued for the first time from 2000 onward. The regressions include all countries in the sample. Appendix B provides a complete list of countries. The number of firms used in these regressions (averaged across the time horizons) is 40,439 in the case of new participants and 1,245 in the case of the top 10 percent most active 1990s participants. MRK = marginal return to capital.

FIGURE 4.5

Effects of Issuance Activity on the MRK Are Stronger in Low-Income Countries Than In Middle-Income Countries

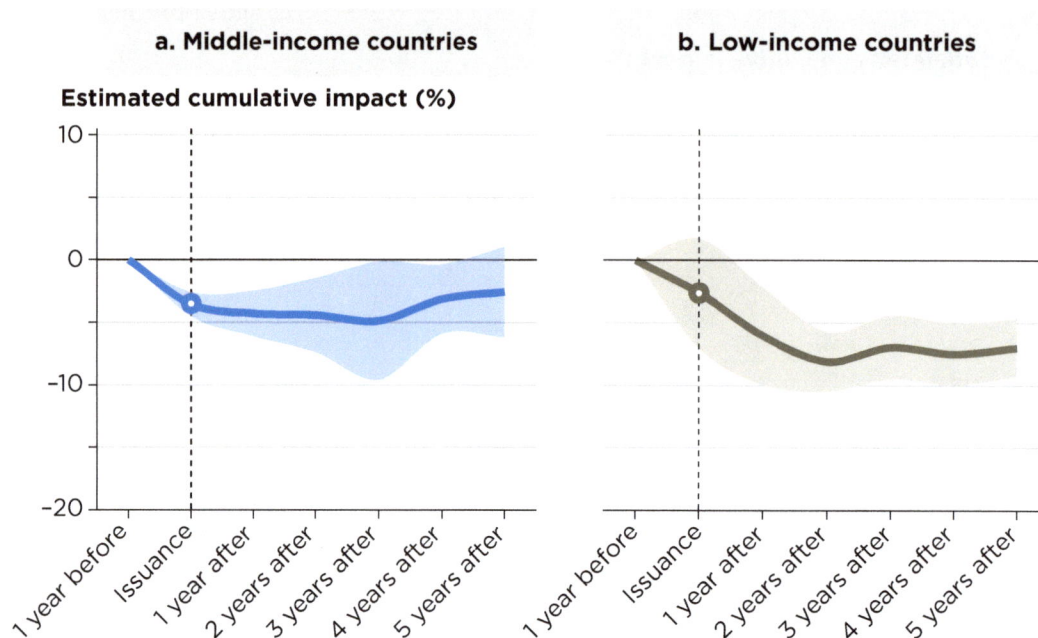

a. Middle-income countries　　　　**b. Low-income countries**

Estimated cumulative impact (%)

Sources: Calculations using issuance data from the Securities Data Company Platinum database and firm balance sheet data from Worldscope, both from LSEG. Appendix K provides details.

Note: This figure shows the estimated cumulative impact (in percentages) of a firm's issuance in the year of issuance (*t* = 0) and in the following five years as well as its 95 percent confidence intervals for MRK. Panels a and b show the results for middle-income countries and low-income countries, respectively. The baseline for estimating cumulative impact is the year before issuance. The number of firms used in these regressions (averaged across the time horizons) is 5,690 in the case of low-income countries and 10,240 in the case of middle-income countries. Appendix B provides the list of countries, grouped by income category. MRK = marginal return to capital.

What Are the Effects by the Type of Instrument and Market?

As shown in the preceding chapters, domestic capital markets accounted for most of the cumulative new issuance over 1990–2022. In addition, both equity and bond issuances were relevant in accounting for those new issuances.

The following analysis aims to determine whether the issuance of securities, equity, or bonds in domestic or international markets was associated with different trajectories in firm performance. To that end, an analysis like the one above was conducted, differentiating between various types of episodes.

For domestic versus foreign markets, physical capital, sales, employment, and MRK trajectories were almost identical after an issuance episode. For physical capital, for example, an issuance is associated with an increase in impact of 10 percent to 11 percent for the two types of markets (table 4.2). However, the average size of issuances is smaller in domestic markets than in foreign markets (US$220 million versus US$390 million), suggesting a stronger effect per dollar of domestically issued securities on firm performance.

In contrast, for equity versus bonds, the effects of an issuance episode are qualitatively similar but quantitatively distinct. Qualitatively, firm sales, physical capital, and employment increase after issuance activity, whereas MRK decreases. On the size of the associations, equity issuances are associated more strongly with these variables than with bond issuances. For physical capital, for example, equity issuances are associated with an increase in impact of 13 percent, compared with an increase of 5 percent for bond issuances (table 4.2). The effects are stronger for equity, even though bond issuances are larger on average (US$113 million for equity versus US$420 million for bonds). These findings are robust to focusing on new participants only and to restricting the episodes to first issuances. These results are similar to what previous studies have found and consistent with the idea that firms with valuable growth opportunities may prefer, on the margin, to issue equity over bonds (Didier et al. 2021; Hovakimian, Hovakimian, and Tehranian 2004).

TABLE 4.2

The Effects Vary by Type of Instrument and Market

	Bonds	Equity	Domestic	Foreign
Sales	0.03 [0.01, 0.04]	0.07 [0.05, 0.09]	0.06 [0.04, 0.07]	0.06 [0.03, 0.08]
Physical capital	0.05 [0.03, 0.07]	0.13 [0.08, 0.17]	0.11 [0.07, 0.15]	0.10 [0.07, 0.12]
Employ-ment	0.03 [0.01, 0.05]	0.07 [0.05, 0.09]	0.06 [0.04, 0.08]	0.05 [0.03, 0.07]
MRK	-0.02 [-0.02, -0.01]	-0.04 [-0.06, -0.02]	-0.04 [-0.06, -0.02]	-0.03 [-0.03, -0.02]

Sources: Calculations using issuance data from the Securities Data Company Platinum database and firm balance sheet data from Worldscope, both from LSEG. Appendix K provides details.

Note: This table shows the estimated impact (in percentages) of a firm's issuance in the year of issuance ($t = 0$) as well as its 95 percent confidence intervals (in squared brackets) for sales, physical capital, employment, and MRK. The effects are estimated restricting the issuance episodes to bond issuances, equity issuances, issuances in the domestic market, and issuances in foreign markets. The regressions include all countries in the sample. Appendix B provides a complete list of countries. The number of firms used in these regressions varies, ranging from 58,228 to 70,700. MRK = marginal return to capital.

What Are the Capital Market Activity and Aggregate Outcomes?

The firm-level evidence in previous sections can be aggregated to examine the impact of capital market financing on economic outcomes at the country level, encompassing all publicly listed firms in a country (appendix N explains the methodology used to construct the aggregate estimates). Similarly, it is also possible to quantify the relative role of new participants.

Physical Capital and Employment

This subsection quantifies the aggregate capital accumulation and employment that followed firms' issuance activity in capital markets in low- and middle-income countries during 2000–22 as well as the relative role of issuances by new participants. As shown in the previous section, issuance activity is estimated to have a positive effect on firms' physical capital and employment and to have an especially strong effect on new participants. Using these estimates and summing across firms' observed issuances during 2000–22, it is possible to calculate the increases in physical capital and employment associated with capital markets activity overall.

Firms' issuance in capital markets was followed by significant capital and labor accumulation over 2000–22 across all country groups. In low-income countries, for example, the estimated impact of firm issuance on cumulative growth in physical capital and labor was 53 percent and 7 percent, respectively (figure 4.6), accounting for around 21 percent and 12 percent, respectively, of the cumulative change measured in the firm balance sheet data during the same period (257 percent and 58 percent). In middle-income countries, the estimated impact of capital markets on cumulative growth in physical capital and labor was 35 percent and 9 percent, representing around 22 percent and 20 percent of the observed increases (158 percent in the case of physical capital and 42 percent in the case of employment). Broadly similar estimated effects apply to high-income countries as well. In the case of China, the impact on capital accumulation was far larger (figure 4.6).

FIGURE 4.6

The Estimated Effects of Capital Market Accounts for a Significant Share of the Observed Cumulative Change (2000–22) in Capital, Employment, and Productivity

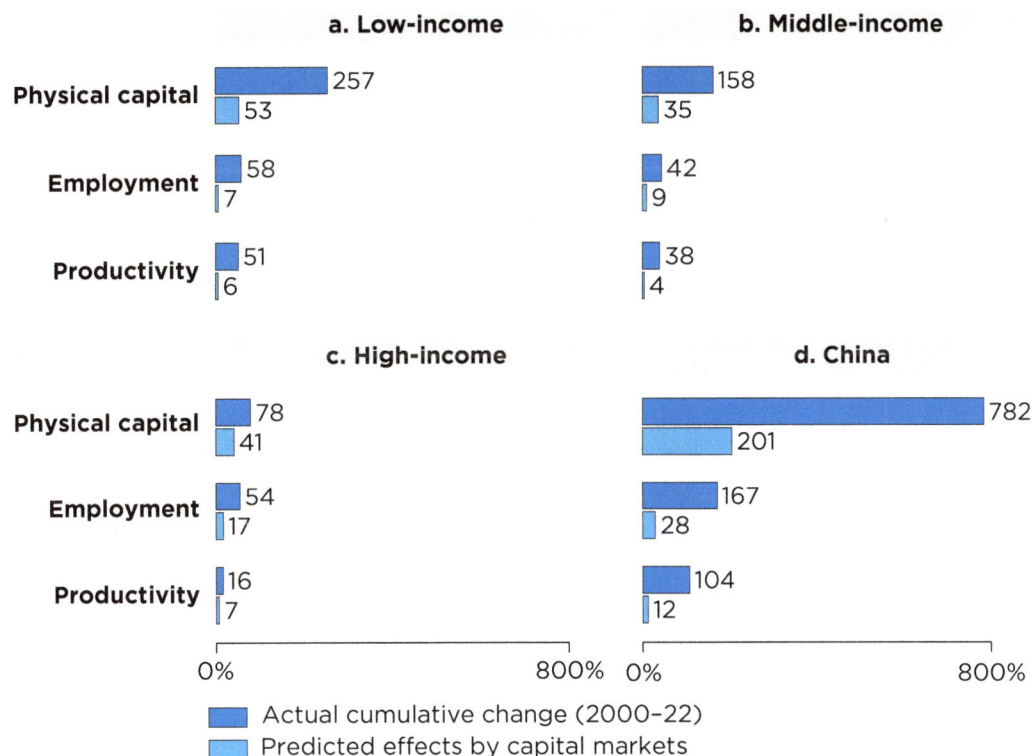

Sources: Calculations using issuance data from the Securities Data Company Platinum database and firm balance sheet data from Worldscope, both from LSEG. Appendix K provides details.
Note: These figures show the cumulative change between 2000 and 2022 in aggregate physical capital, employment, and productivity measured in the Securities Data Company Platinum database-Worldscope sample (dark blue) as well as the estimated impact of firms' issuances on these variables (light blue). Appendix B provides the list of countries, grouped by income category.

New participants accounted for a significant share of the estimated effect of capital markets on physical capital and employment. In low- and middle-income countries as a whole, for instance, new participants accounted for 24 percent and 5 percent of physical capital and employment or 58 percent and 61 percent of the overall estimated impact of capital markets. A sizable relative contribution of new participants is also present when considering low-income countries, China, and middle-income countries separately. In contrast, the relative contribution of new participants was lower in high-income countries, where they accounted for 27 percent and 31 percent of the overall contribution of capital markets to physical capital and employment.

Aggregate Productivity

The change in productivity in a particular industry and country can be expressed as a function of a within-firm component (changes in efficiency within each firm) and a reallocation component (changes in the efficiency with which factors of production are allocated across firms) (Baqaee and Farhi 2019; Bau and Matray 2023; Petrin and Levinsohn 2012). In a context where firms exhibit different levels of MRK, aggregate productivity through the reallocation component will increase if a factor of production (for example, capital) is allocated to firms with a relatively high MRK.[5]

This subsection aims to quantify the extent to which new participants with an ex ante higher MRK and increasing participation in capital markets resulted in aggregate productivity gains via an improved capital allocation. The analysis consists of using the changes in firms' physical capital predicted by capital market activity and firms' initial levels of MRK to estimate the implied changes in aggregate productivity that are due to firms' capital market activity.

Capital market activity, through an improvement in the allocation of capital across firms, was followed by aggregate productivity growth over 2000–22. In low- and middle-income countries as a whole, firms' issuances led to a 5 percentage point increase in aggregate productivity, which represents 11 percent of the increase in aggregate productivity in these country groups over 2000–22 measured in the Securities Data Company Platinum database-Worldscope sample—that is, 43 percent. In middle-income countries, low-income countries, and China, respectively, firms' issuances in capital markets led to a 4, 6, and 12 percentage points increase in aggregate productivity (figure 4.6). These numbers represent 12 percent, 11 percent, and 12 percent, respectively, of the increase in aggregate productivity in these country groups over 2000–22 measured in the Securities Data Company Platinum database-Worldscope sample.

The relative role of new participants was sizable. In low- and middle-income countries, new participants accounted for 58 percent of the estimated impact of capital markets on aggregate productivity. For middle-income countries, low-income countries, and China, new participants accounted for 52 percent, 65 percent, and 84 percent, respectively, of the overall contribution of capital markets. The relative contribution of new participants in high-income countries was significantly lower at 25 percent.

As in many other studies, the analysis here comes with caveats that could be addressed in future research. For example, it has been assumed that firms would not have found alternative sources of financing in the absence of capital markets. However, firms with good business opportunities could have obtained financing through banks and might have exhibited a similar performance. Hence, the actual effects may be smaller than those estimated here. Another caveat is that the estimates refer to the sample of publicly listed firms, which may perform differently from other firms. Furthermore, the methodology applied here abstracts from potential general equilibrium effects such as changes in prices, wages, or interest rates.

Notes

1. The data set used in this chapter is the result of merging information on firms' capital market activity (from Securities Data Company Platinum) with income statement and balance sheet information (from Worldscope). Appendix K describes the data set in more detail.
2. To carry out comparisons within an industry and country, all variables in this section are standardized by subtracting their industry-country means and dividing them by their industry-country standard deviation.
3. Because these numbers show the location of different types of firms in their industry-country distribution, they are not comparable across country groups. However, it is possible to compare the differences between types of firms across country groups.
4. All unreported results in the book are available upon request.
5. This book abstracts from changes in the within-firm component, mainly due to data limitations. Computing physical efficiency at the firm level requires information on firms' prices, which is not available in Worldscope.

References

Asker, J., A. Collard-Wexler, and J. de Loecker. 2014. "Dynamic Inputs and Resource (Mis) Allocation." *Journal of Political Economy* 122 (5): 1013–63.

Baqaee, D. R., and E. Farhi. 2019. "A Short Note on Aggregating Productivity." NBER Working Paper 25688, National Bureau of Economic Research, Cambridge, MA.

Bau, N., and A. Matray. 2023. "Misallocation and Capital Market Integration: Evidence from India." *Econometrica* 91 (1): 67–106.

Cohen, W. 2010. "Fifty Years of Empirical Studies of Innovative Activity and Performance." In *Handbook of Economics and Innovation*, edited by B. H. Hall and N. Rosenberg. Amsterdam: North Holland Elsevier.

David, J. M., H. A. Hopenhayn, and V. Venkateswaran. 2016. "Information, Misallocation, and Aggregate Productivity." *Quarterly Journal of Economics* 131 (2): 943–1005.

David, J. M., L. Schmid, and D. Zeke. 2022. "Risk-Adjusted Capital Allocation and Misallocation." *Journal of Financial Economics* 145 (3): 684–705.

Didier, T., R. Levine, R. Llovet Montanes, and S. Schmukler. 2021. "Capital Market Financing and Firm Growth." *Journal of International Money and Finance* 118 (November): 102459.

Ferreira, M. H., T. Haber, and C. Rorig. 2023. "Financial Constraints and Firm Size: Micro-Evidence and Aggregate Implications." DNB Working Paper 777, De Nederlandsche Bank, Amsterdam.

Gertler, M., and S. Gilchrist. 1994. "Monetary Policy, Business Cycles, and the Behavior of Small Manufacturing Firms." *Quarterly Journal of Economics* 59 (2): 309–40.

Gopinath, G., S. Kalemli-Ozcan, L. Karabarbounis, and C. Villegas-Sanchez. 2017. "Capital Allocation and Productivity in South Europe." *Quarterly Journal of Economics* 132 (4): 1915–67.

Hovakimian, A., G. Hovakimian, and H. Tehranian. 2004. "Determinants of Target Capital Structure: The Case of Dual Debt and Equity Issues." *Journal of Financial Economics* 71 (3): 517–40.

Jordà, O. 2005. "Estimation and Inference of Impulse Responses by Local Projections." *American Economic Review* 95 (1): 161–82.

Levinsohn, J., and A. Petrin. 2003. "Estimating Production Functions Using Inputs to Control for Unobservables." *Review of Economic Studies* 70 (2): 317–41.

Petrin, A., and J. Levinsohn. 2012. "Measuring Aggregate Productivity Growth Using Plant-Level Data." *RAND Journal of Economics* 43 (4): 705–25.

CHAPTER 5

Drivers of Capital Market Growth and Policy Implications

Alvaro Pedraza and Imtiaz Ul Haq

Key Messages

- Higher capital issuance is strongly and positively correlated with economic growth, accounting for nearly half of the variation across countries.

- Policies to increase investable savings, such as pension reforms and international capital account liberalization, are followed by greater issuance.

- Policies to improve financial intermediation are also associated with higher capital market financing, including developing a yield curve through sovereign issuances, strengthening investor protection, and improving the information environment.

- Sustained capital market development requires a series of multifaceted policy reforms rather than isolated initiatives.

This chapter explores potential drivers behind the expansion of capital market activity in low- and middle-income countries. It studies how net capital issuances relate to aggregate economic activity and how policies can spur firm fundraising in these markets. The policies are classified as those that *increase investable savings* and those that *improve financial intermediation*.

The first category includes policies to expand the overall supply of capital. The second category focuses on policies to facilitate the transfer of funds from investors to firms, such as measures that lower information costs, transaction costs, and investor risks. Reducing such frictions makes it easier for investors to allocate capital and for firms to access financing.[1]

Previous evidence suggests that sustained capital market development requires comprehensive domestic reforms that encompass a broad set of policy measures rather than isolated initiatives. The chapter concludes by proposing a research agenda that builds on the findings in the book, offering pathways for further development of capital markets in low- and middle-income countries.

Understanding the Role of Capital Markets and Economic Growth

A natural starting point for understanding the documented expansion of capital markets in low- and middle-income countries is to consider the relationship between these markets and economic activity. As chapter 4 highlights, growth in capital market fundraising is strongly correlated with capital accumulation, employment growth, and productivity gains, which subsequently boost economic activity.[2] However, this relationship is not one-way, as economic growth is also expected to contribute to deepening capital markets through various channels.

For firms, economic growth expands business opportunities and, as these arise, the demand for external financing increases. Although bank credit often serves as a primary source of funding, it may not always be the most suitable option. Firms requiring large-scale investments, those engaged in riskier ventures, or those with projects involving long-term capital commitments might find that issuing bonds or equity in capital markets offers a more effective or suitable funding option.

When the economy grows, households have more disposable income, which can boost domestic savings. In turn, these savings provide a larger pool of capital that can be channeled into productive investments in capital markets. Moreover, countries with strong economic outlooks are likely to attract foreign investors. An influx of foreign capital further strengthens the supply side of the market, offering local firms additional resources to finance their growth.

In line with these arguments, countries with the highest gross domestic product (GDP) growth rates also experience the largest increase in capital market activity (figure 5.1). The growth of cumulative net capital issuance (CNI) in low- and middle-income countries has surpassed that of high-income countries and is strongly associated with economic growth in the 2000s. High-income countries have grown at an average annual rate of 1.3 percent, while low- and middle-income countries have grown at 3.2 percent. Correspondingly, the average annual growth in CNI was 4.9 percent in high-income countries and 6.0 percent in low- and middle-income countries. In essence, the convergence in fundraising on capital markets between country income groups largely reflects a convergence in economic growth.

FIGURE 5.1

Growth of GDP and Growth of CNI Are Strongly Correlated

CNI growth (median 2000–22)

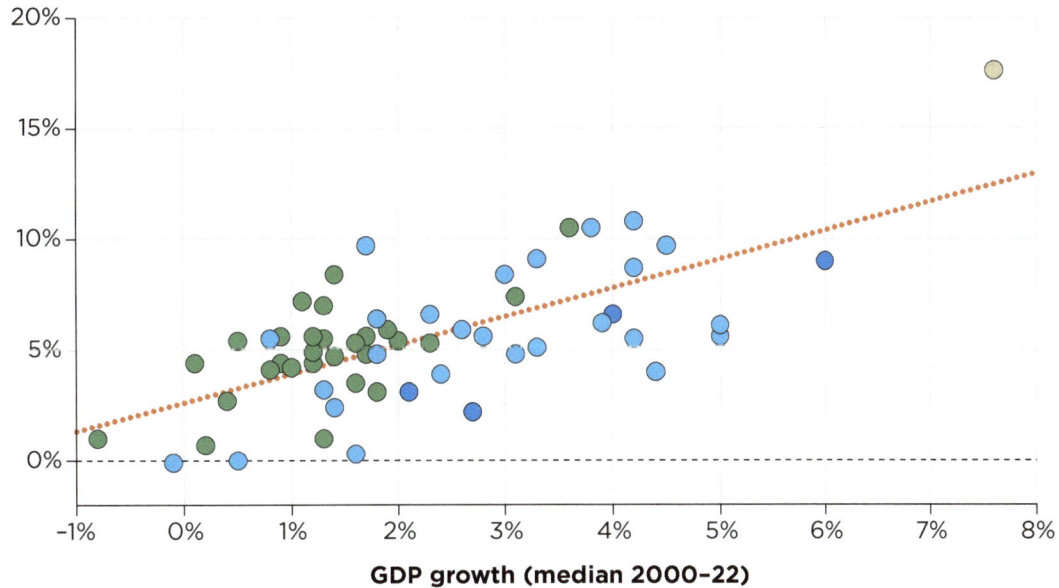

GDP growth (median 2000–22)

● Low-income countries ● Middle-income countries ○ China ● High-income countries

Sources: Calculations using issuance data from the Securities Data Company Platinum database from LSEG and GDP data from the World Bank's World Development Indicators.

Note: The figure presents the correlation between yearly growth in CNI among nonfinancial firms and country GDP growth rate. CNI for year *Y* is computed as the sum of equity and bond issuance (minus bonds that matured) between 1990 and year *Y*. For each country, the median of the yearly CNI growth and GDP growth for the sample period are plotted, with the regression line depicted by a dotted line. Only countries with issuance activity in at least 50 percent of the sample years (2000–22) are included. The slope and *R*-squared when China is included in sample are 1.25 and 0.45, respectively. Appendix B provides the list of countries, grouped by income category. CNI = cumulative net capital issuance; GDP = gross domestic product.

Effective macroeconomic and growth policies can lead to capital market expansion by fostering a stable environment that increases investable savings and creates opportunities for firms. Past studies suggest that economic development and growth (in both level and growth of GDP) and macroeconomic stability are essential for capital market development (BIS 2019; Carvajal et al. 2019). In particular, high levels of domestic savings and investment rates, a strong current account balance, and stable inflation and exchange rates can promote capital market growth (World Bank 2020a). These factors can engender a virtuous cycle whereby economic growth and capital market development reinforce each other.

Overall, the increase in CNI is associated with economic growth, with nearly half of the variation across countries over the past two decades attributed to GDP growth. This strong correlation underscores the role of economic activity in shaping capital markets. As the slope of the regression exceeds 1, most countries may be expected to see an increase in the ratio of issuance to GDP, consistent with results from previous chapters, which show that issuance has grown faster than GDP. The remainder of the chapter explores the role of select policies that may contribute to the expansion of capital market financing beyond economic growth, with a focus on low- and middle-income countries.

Growing Investable Savings

Institutional investors are a major catalyst for the supply side of capital markets, enabling the pooling of risks for individual investors. Their ability to process information and transact in larger volumes also reduces the cost of intermediation, benefiting both investors and issuers. Institutional investors with long-term investment horizons, such as pension funds and insurance companies, contribute to developing longer-term securities markets. They also promote better transparency and governance, improve market microstructure, and support adopting innovative financial products (Boone and White 2015; Lewellen and Lewellen 2022).

Implementing Pension Reforms

One prominent example of institutional investor development is the growth of pension funds. Pension reforms, often driven by the need to address the financial instability of pay-as-you-go systems due to political and demographic pressures, have contributed to the development of pension funds. Following the experience in Chile, several countries in Latin America and Central and Eastern Europe adopted variants of funded, privately managed, defined-contribution accounts as part of their retirement systems. As figure 5.2 shows, countries that implemented these reforms saw a marked increase in domestic issuance activity (adjusting for GDP).[3]

FIGURE 5.2

Countries with Pension Reforms Experienced Higher CNI in Domestic Markets

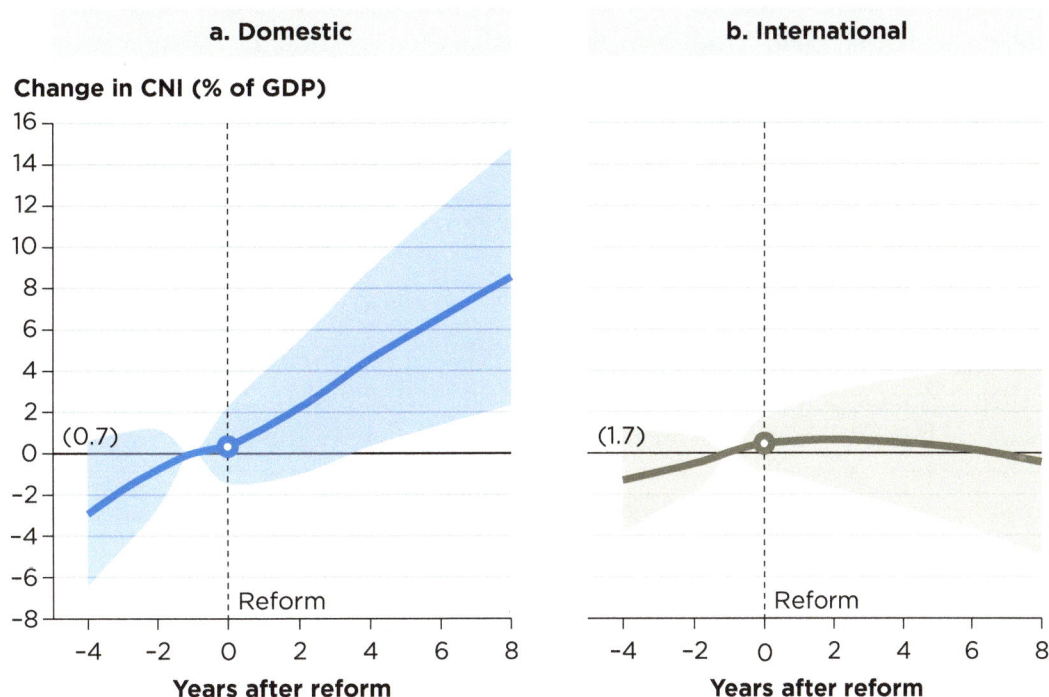

a. Domestic

Change in CNI (% of GDP)

b. International

Sources: Calculations using data from the Securities Data Company Platinum database from LSEG and the International Federation of Pension Fund Administrators and GDP data from the World Bank's World Development Indicators.

Note: The sample includes 30 low- and middle-income countries with pension reforms introducing mandatory or quasi-mandatory individually funded programs between 1990 and 2022. The figure illustrates the impact of major pension reforms on domestic (panel a) and foreign (panel b) issuance activity, beyond what would be expected in a counterfactual drawing on a control group consisting of 117 countries from various income groups that did not implement major pension reforms during the sample period. The event year is defined as the year when the first major pension reform was implemented in each country. The vertical axis shows the total change of CNI as a proportion of GDP relative to the year before the reform. The ratio of CNI to GDP for year Y is computed as the sum of equity and bond issuance (minus bonds that matured) between 1990 and year Y, divided by GDP in year Y. In the baseline year ($t = -1$), domestic and foreign CNI were 0.7 percent and 1.7 percent of GDP, respectively. Point estimates are presented with 95 percent confidence intervals, controlling for year and country fixed effects. CNI = cumulative net capital issuance; GDP = gross domestic product.

Specifically, in the year before implementing these pension reforms, the average CNI in domestic markets was around 0.7 percent of GDP. Estimates based on an event study approach indicate that within four years of implementing the reforms, domestic CNI in these countries increased by 3.2 percent of GDP, or 4.6 times the prereform level.[4] This is a substantial increase over countries that did not undertake such reforms. In contrast, there was no notable difference in foreign issuance activity between firms in countries with pension reforms and those without, suggesting that the reforms primarily promoted domestic capital markets.

The positive effects of pension reforms on domestic issuance activity appear to have been persistent, with positive impacts over the first decade after implementation. In most cases, these pension systems are still in their early accumulation stages, and overall domestic savings continue to grow, which is expected to expand financing further for firms in capital markets. The fact that the increase in CNI postreform occurred in domestic markets aligns with the expectation that local investors prefer to invest domestically (due to "home bias") or are forced to do so by regulation (for example, limits on the foreign allocation of pension fund portfolios). Therefore, such reforms can be especially beneficial for small, financially constrained firms unable to access international capital markets. Relatedly, the growth in domestic issuances postreform was driven largely by firms without previous issuance activity. There is no indication that firms already accessing international markets shifted to domestic ones. Instead, the reforms expanded access to financing in domestic markets for a broader range of companies, enabling more firms to benefit from the increasing pool of capital available locally.

In figure 5.2, it appears that countries with pension reforms experienced an increase in domestic issuances even before the reform was enacted officially, although this increase is not statistically significant. This increase could reflect anticipation effects, where firms may have expected that the reform would increase the supply of capital in the domestic market and positioned themselves accordingly. Additionally, complementary policies introduced prior to pension reforms also may have stimulated domestic capital markets. Although other contributing factors cannot be ruled out, placebo tests—where control countries were "treated" as if they had implemented similar reforms——show that the substantial increase in domestic issuance activity in the decade following reform is uniquely observed in countries that implemented pension reforms (appendix O), highlighting the link between the strengthening of the domestic investor base and the expansion of domestic capital markets.

These results are corroborated by other studies, which considered portfolio holdings and auction data from primary issuances in Chile, providing direct evidence that institutional investors contribute to the development of domestic debt markets. For instance, pension funds hold an average of 40 percent of outstanding domestic corporate debt and, along with insurance companies, are the largest bidders for domestic government debt (Opazo, Raddatz, and Schmukler 2015).[5]

The findings here do not imply that policy makers should favor pension systems based on defined-contribution and privately managed pension accounts. Fiscal, equity, and social considerations also determine the appropriate type of pension system in a country. However, evidence suggests that reforms based on private capitalization, which have supported the growth of institutional investors, have contributed to the development of domestic capital markets. Strategies aimed at boosting domestic savings, combined with professional management, could have similar effects, particularly in countries where domestic institutional investors are still nascent or emerging.

Enacting Liberalization Policies

Another approach to increasing the pool of investable savings is to enact liberalization policies. These measures—such as reducing capital controls and opening markets to foreign investors—allow firms to access a broader range of funding sources. Liberalization gained popularity in the 1990s as a mechanism to stimulate economic growth, attract foreign investment, and integrate low- and middle-income economies into the global market.

Figure 5.3 illustrates the changes in corporate debt issuance (adjusting for GDP) in both domestic and foreign markets around recent liberalization events in low- and middle-income countries.[6] These events are identified using the Chinn-Ito index, a commonly used measure of capital account openness (Chinn and Ito 2008). A liberalization event is defined as a year in which a country exhibits a substantial increase in the index since the year 2000.[7] The sample consists of 15 country-year events, including significant policy changes such as the elimination of restrictions on capital inflows, a country's entry into the eurozone, the introduction of regional economic partnerships, and the removal of barriers to foreign ownership of domestic securities.[8]

Firms in countries that adopted these liberalization policies increased their bond issuance activity in international markets. In particular, the ratio of CNI to GDP rose to 2.4 percent within four years of liberalization, compared with an average of 1.3 percent in the year prior to the policy—an estimated 84 percent growth in international bond issuances associated with the liberalization measures. However, there is no evidence that these policies led to an increase in corporate fundraising activity in local debt markets, suggesting that, rather than directing foreign capital into domestic markets, these liberalization measures primarily enabled firms to raise funds through international bond issuances.

Corporate debt placements tend to be significantly larger in foreign markets than in domestic markets. As documented in chapter 3, the average size of foreign bond issuances was three times the size of domestic bond issuances in the period between 2010 and 2022. Therefore, large corporations with the capacity to engage in foreign markets likely captured the most direct benefits from these liberalization policies.

FIGURE 5.3

Firms in Countries That Liberalized the International Capital Account Issued More Foreign Bonds

| a. Domestic debt | b. International debt |

Change in CNI (% of GDP)

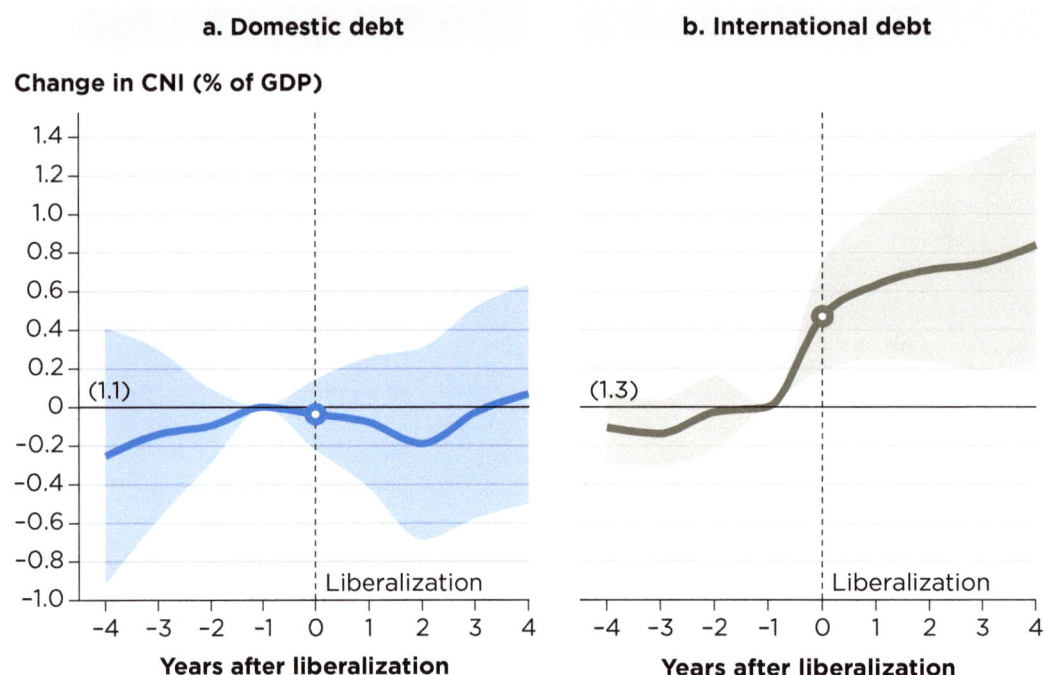

Sources: Calculations using data from the Securities Data Company Platinum database from LSEG and Chinn-Ito databases and GDP data from the World Bank's World Development Indicators.

Note: The figure examines the impact of 15 major liberalization episodes in low- and middle-income countries between 2000 and 2021. Major liberalization episodes are defined as an increase of more than 1.5 standard deviations in a country's Chinn-Ito index. The figure illustrates the impact of such events on domestic (panel a) and foreign (panel b) issuance activity, beyond what would be expected in a counterfactual drawing on a control group consisting of 132 countries from various income groups that did not experience such an event between 2000 and 2021. The event year is defined as the year of the major liberalization episode in each country. The vertical axis shows the total change in CNI as a proportion of GDP relative to the year before the liberalization episode. The ratio of CNI to GDP for year Y is computed as the sum of equity and bond issuance (minus bonds that matured) between 1990 and year Y, divided by GDP in year Y. In the baseline year ($t = -1$), domestic CNI and foreign CNI were 1.1 percent and 1.3 percent of GDP, respectively. Point estimates are presented with 95 percent confidence intervals, controlling for year and country fixed effects. CNI = cumulative net capital issuance; GDP = gross domestic product.

Previous studies have suggested that international capital account liberalizations might in some cases have the strongest impact on firm financing in local markets with an established, robust base of domestic investors. According to Cortina et al. (2024), China's market internationalization after 2012 led to a substantial rise in equity financing, but this growth was fueled largely by domestic investors. As foreign ownership restrictions on some firms were lifted, domestic investors bought shares in anticipation of future demand from foreign investors. This sequence suggests that a well-developed base of local investors is crucial to leveraging the full benefits of liberalization for firm financing.

The policies discussed in this section point to two key implications:

- *Development of domestic investors.* Policies aimed at growing the base of domestic investors have a direct impact on the development of domestic capital markets. These strategies tend to support a broader range of firms, particularly smaller corporations among those issuing, that might not meet the scale requirements for participating in international markets.

- *Impact of international capital account liberalization.* Policies that facilitate the flow of capital across borders seem to benefit large domestic firms, enabling them to access and issue debt more easily in foreign markets. However, such policies do not necessarily attract foreign investors to the host country's markets.

Overall, promoting institutional investors and capital account liberalization contributes to capital market development but benefits different types of firms. Policies aimed at growing domestic investors can support small and mid-size firms, while liberalization policies favor larger firms that can meet the demands of issuing in international markets. Scale-related challenges arise in two main ways. First, due to high fixed transaction costs in international markets (such as the cost of obtaining a credit rating from a global agency), small issuances may be less attractive for investment banks to facilitate. Second, international investors face significant hurdles when participating in small issuance sizes or small companies. The need to establish a local presence and acquire detailed knowledge of domestic firms is costly, making participation in some issuances uneconomical. For example, global asset managers report that issuances below US$50 million are unprofitable, which limits the interest of foreign investors (Demekas and Nerlich 2020). In contrast, domestic investors, who generally incur a lower cost for acquiring information, are more inclined to participate in small issuances, thus supporting local market activity.

Improving Financial Intermediation

To facilitate the transfer of funds from investors to firms, policies can aim to reduce information costs, transaction costs, and risks to investors. Doing so can increase issuances in domestic capital markets, especially in low- and middle-income countries, where these issues tend to be more pronounced. Measures to improve intermediation may include developing pricing benchmarks, strengthening investor protection, and improving the disclosure environment.

Developing Pricing Benchmarks

Regular and standardized issuance of government debt across a range of maturities is important for developing a functioning domestic bond market. By establishing a consistent issuance schedule, the government can create a market environment that encourages the entry of new investors, including foreign participants, and improve overall market liquidity.

Issuing government bonds to set benchmarks for various maturities—such as 1, 2, 5, and 10 years—helps to establish a yield curve that serves as a reference point for pricing other domestic currency instruments. This yield curve is useful for pricing risk and facilitating the extension of maturities for various financial products, contributing to the development of a more mature bond market.

There is, however, concern that public debt could crowd out private debt, drawing investors away from corporate bonds. Despite this concern, according to investors' surveys, developing a public debt market is often viewed as a necessary step for the emergence of a corporate bond market (Demekas and Nerlich 2020).

Figure 5.4 illustrates the relationship between the year a country first began regularly issuing sovereign bonds and the year when corporations first issued bonds in the domestic market. The data suggest that establishing a government bond market creates a framework that corporate issuers can use later. In this manner, government debt issuance precedes the development of a corporate bond market.[9]

Without a developed local government bond market, corporations may issue bonds but are often forced to do so in international markets, issuing in foreign currency under the rules of the host market. As discussed in this book, such access is generally limited to the largest corporations, leaving smaller domestic firms without viable options for bond financing. A well-functioning domestic government bond market is therefore important for improving access for these firms.

FIGURE 5.4

Issuing Sovereign Bonds Has Generally Preceded Developing the Domestic Corporate Bond Market

Countries with first corporate bond issuance after 1995

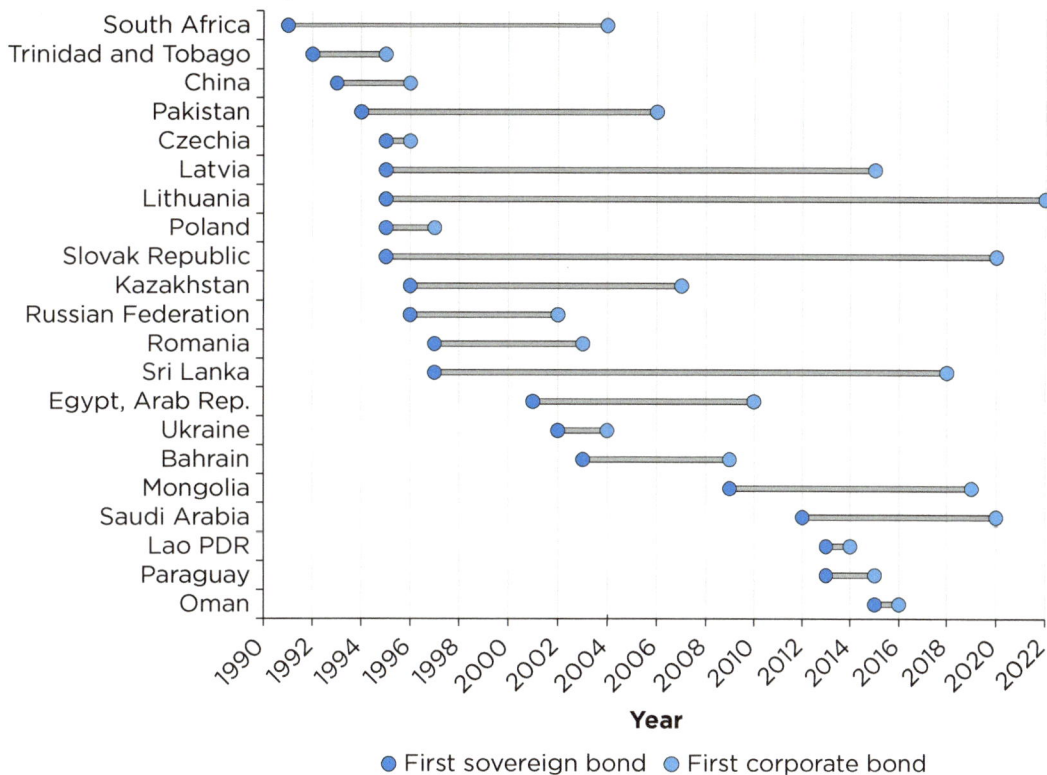

● First sovereign bond   ● First corporate bond

Source: Calculations using data from the Securities Data Company Platinum database from LSEG.

Note: The figure shows the first year that nonfinancial firms issued bonds in the domestic market and the first year of domestic sovereign bond issuance. The sample includes low- and middle-income countries where the first corporate domestic bond issuance occurred in 1995 or later. Appendix B provides the list of countries, grouped by income category.

Strengthening Investor Protection

Legal protection of investors is critical for investor participation in capital markets—to ensure their contractual and property rights. Shareholder protections are important for equity markets, while credit rights and bankruptcy laws are relevant for bond markets. Of particular relevance is the treatment of minority shareholders by controlling shareholders, a prominent corporate governance issue for investors in low- and middle-income countries (IFC 2018). Appropriate regulation can mitigate this and other agency issues, for example, by encouraging independent and strong boards of directors via measures such as requiring separation of the chief executive officer and board chairperson, independent nonexecutive directors, and board audit committees. During 2014–20, 31 countries enhanced investor protection policies related to these issues, of which 25 were low- and middle-income countries and China.

Such shareholder protection policies are associated with higher domestic equity issuances, adjusting for GDP (figure 5.5).[10] Therefore, regulatory requirements or incentives to reduce agency issues can promote capital market development. Such policies do not appear to have a significant impact on foreign equity issues (unreported results), likely because such firms are required to meet the corporate governance standards of the foreign market regardless of the domestic environment. Nor do they tend to significantly influence debt issuances (unreported results), since shareholder and bondholder protection policies are distinct.

Domestic policies can set minimum corporate governance standards for local equity issuers, although firms are free to follow higher standards voluntarily. For example, the introduction of Brazil's alternative stock exchange Novo Mercado, where firms voluntarily follow higher corporate governance standards, was related to higher issuance volumes (box 5.1).

FIGURE 5.5

Better Corporate Governance Standards Are Related to Higher Domestic Equity Issuances

Domestic equity (CNI to GDP)

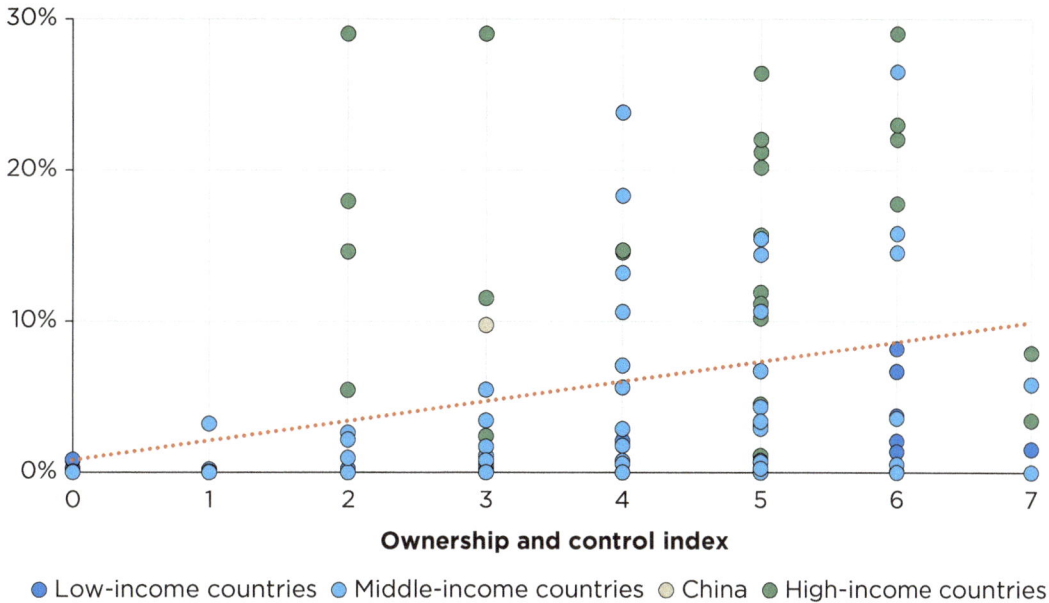

Ownership and control index

● Low-income countries ○ Middle-income countries ○ China ● High-income countries

Sources: Calculations using data from the Securities Data Company Platinum database from LSEG and World Bank *Doing Business 2020* (Work Bank 2020b) databases and GDP data from the World Bank's World Development Indicators.

Note: This figure plots the correlation between CNI of domestic equity (as a ratio to domestic GDP) and a measure of shareholder protection. The ratio of CNI of domestic equity to GDP for a country for year *Y* is computed as the sum of all domestic equity issuances between 1990 and year *Y*, divided by the country's GDP in year *Y*. The measure of shareholder protection is an index ranging from 0 to 7 (higher numbers indicating stronger protection) based on regulations requiring corporate governance safeguards that protect shareholders from undue board control and managerial entrenchment; this measure comes from the variable "extent of ownership and control index" from the World Bank *Doing Business 2020* (World Bank 2020b). Data for the shareholder protection index are only available for 2014–20 (both inclusive), and at least three observations are needed for a country to be included in the sample. For both annual variables, the median values are plotted for each country for 2014–20. The dotted line depicts the regression slope for these datapoints (including China), which is significantly different from zero at the 5 percent level. Appendix B provides the list of countries, grouped by income category. CNI = cumulative net capital issuance; GDP = gross domestic product.

BOX 5.1

Brazil's Novo Mercado Stock Exchange

The Novo Mercado is a special segment of the Brazil Stock Exchange. It was created in 2000 to allow firms to adhere voluntarily to higher corporate governance standards. It also disallows dual-share classes, providing greater protection for minority shareholders by giving each share equal voting rights.

It was expected that investors would perceive firms choosing to list on the Novo Mercado instead of the main exchange to be less risky, given their voluntary adoption of higher standards of corporate governance in a jurisdiction with relatively weak governance legislation and institutions. These higher standards were expected to attract greater investor interest and a higher share price, lowering the cost of issuance for firms and sparking growth in the country's relatively inactive equity market (World Bank 2008).

The launch of the Novo Mercado was indeed followed by an uptick in stock market activity in Brazil. There were both an initial wave of initial public offerings (IPOs) from 2004 to 2007 and a wave of secondary offerings from 2009 to 2011 (CFA 2017). Much of this activity was on the Novo Mercado exchange, which, by 2007, hosted 81 of Brazil's 113 IPOs (Stewart 2010). By 2017, the Novo Mercado exchange represented close to 40 percent of the total number of listed firms and market capitalization in Brazil.

Widespread use of the Novo Mercado exchange, with its international-style corporate governance standards, likely helped to draw in new sources of capital. Foreign investors purchased more than 70 percent of shares in new listings. Furthermore, more than half of IPOs were in sectors not previously listed on the Brazilian stock exchange, suggesting that the voluntary corporate governance exchange may have contributed to growth in the number of firms participating in the stock market (World Bank 2008).

Previous studies have suggested that the effect of corporate governance on firms' access to capital market financing is more pronounced in markets with weak investor protection (Chen, Chen, and Wei 2009). This effect is particularly true for firms with good investment opportunities, including new participants with a high marginal return to capital (MRK). Improved corporate governance has also been documented to reduce the transaction costs of issuing equity (Chen, Goyal, and Zolotoy 2022). Even so, corporate governance is, on average, lower in markets with weak legal systems, underscoring the need for firms in low- and middle-income countries to make such improvements (Klapper and Love 2004). In particular, state- and family-owned firms in low- and middle-income countries tend to exhibit weaker corporate governance and may benefit most from undertaking such measures (Lima and Sanvicente 2013).

Strong legal and regulatory frameworks must be accompanied by adequate enforcement capacity to ensure investor rights. Governments should ensure that regulators have sufficient independence, budget, and technical capacity to fulfill their functions. Research shows that better enforcement capacity enhances the effects of regulations on capital markets (Christensen, Hail, and Leuz 2016).

Improving Disclosure Environment

Policies that improve disclosure by firms can lower information acquisition costs and expropriation risks for investors, thus attracting more funds to capital markets and encouraging issuances by firms (Khurana Pereira, and Martin 2006). Figure 5.6 underscores this relationship, depicting a positive and significant correlation between disclosure requirements for publicly listed firms and domestic equity issuances (adjusting for GDP). This relationship also holds for domestic bond issuances (unreported results), suggesting that debt and equity investors alike benefit from more firm disclosure.

Disclosure policies aim to improve the quantity, quality, and timeliness of material information disclosed by firms. The analysis in figure 5.6 focuses on regulations related to corporate disclosure around ownership stakes, compensation, audits, and financial prospects.[11] Policies on this front may include regulatory requirements for annual financial statements to be externally audited, prompt disclosure of significant ownership stakes, making managerial compensation public, and disclosing more information on corporations' board members. Several countries strengthened such disclosure policies during 2014–20, including 27 low- and middle-income countries.

FIGURE 5.6

Better Disclosure Is Correlated with More Domestic Equity Issuance

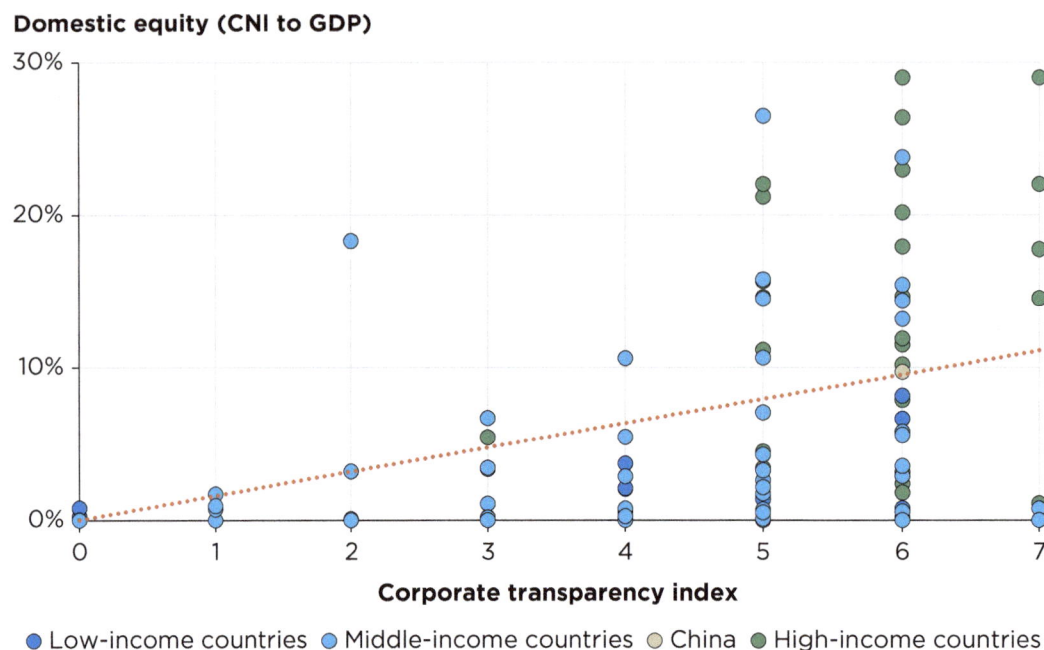

Domestic equity (CNI to GDP)

Low-income countries   Middle-income countries   China   High-income countries

Corporate transparency index

Sources: Calculations using data from the Securities Data Company Platinum database from LSEG and World Bank *Doing Business 2020* (World Bank 2020b) databases and GDP data from the World Bank's World Development Indicators.

Note: This figure plots the correlation between CNI of domestic equity (as a ratio to domestic GDP) and a measure of corporate disclosure. CNI of domestic equity as a ratio to GDP for a country for year Y is computed as the sum of all domestic equity issuances between 1990 and year Y, divided by the country's GDP in year Y. The measure of corporate disclosure is an index ranging from 0 to 7 (higher numbers indicating more disclosure) based on regulation related to corporate disclosure; this measure comes from the variable "extent of corporate transparency index" from the World Bank *Doing Business 2020* (World Bank 2020b). Data for this variable are available only for 2014–20 (both inclusive), and at least three observations are needed for a country to be included in the sample. For both annual variables, the median values are plotted for each country for 2014–20. The dotted line depicts the regression slope for these datapoints (including China), which is significantly different from zero at the 5 percent level. Appendix B provides the list of countries, grouped by income category. CNI = cumulative net capital issuance; GDP = gross domestic product.

Policy makers can also improve the domestic information environment by supporting third-party information providers such as credit rating agencies and research analysis firms. In particular, domestic third-party information providers often have better access to and better understanding of local information than their global counterparts, making them better placed to improve transparency in domestic markets, especially for more opaque issuances, including by new participants (Butler 2008). More recently, some stock exchanges, such as the Shanghai Stock Exchange, have established innovative two-way interactive communication platforms that allow firms to respond to specific information requests by investors. Customized information flows are valued by investors and help to improve firms' access to capital market financing. Firms can further improve the information environment by voluntarily disclosing high-quality information beyond that required by regulations.

Effective disclosure regulations, however, need to balance the trade-off between investor protection and higher costs to issuers, given that disclosure costs are among the main regulatory costs for publicly listed firms. Small firms can be more sensitive to such costs; exemptions could thus apply for firms below a certain size. For example, regulation could allow for a "ramp up" period where small firms are given a certain time frame in which to abide by the full disclosure schedule following an initial public offering. For secondary issuances by listed firms, allowing shelf-registered equity offerings or exempting the need to produce a prospectus for small firms can reduce their issuance costs. Relatedly, policy makers can consider segmented stock exchanges for small and medium enterprises, which have lower regulatory and issuance requirements than main exchanges, thus reducing the entry barriers for small firms (including new participants).

The disclosure policies discussed in this analysis complement policies on investor protection outlined previously, reducing the expropriation risk for investors. So, it is not surprising that measures capturing such policies are highly correlated (with a 0.75 correlation coefficient), suggesting that policy makers tend to adopt a comprehensive approach to investor protection. Such policy making may cover several related aspects (such as greater liability of directors and facilitating shareholder litigation). These policies do not appear to influence international issuances as much, likely because such issuances are subject to the regulations of the foreign market regardless of the domestic environment.

Wider Reforms Are Needed

Appropriate policies can accelerate capital market growth, extending beyond those described above. However, sustained capital market development requires a series of reforms, rather than a single policy. For example, East Asian markets expanded rapidly following several reforms after the 1997–98 Asian financial crisis, which included liberalizing foreign exchange administration rules, improving the regulatory framework, strengthening domestic market infrastructure, and creating transparent and credible bond indexes (Packer and Remolona 2012). A broad range of policies that target gaps in the domestic environment is thus essential to promote issuances.

The specific policy mix for each country often depends on its context. Not all growing markets undertook the same reforms, nor were there clear patterns in the sequencing of reforms (Abraham, Cortina, and Schmukler 2021). For example, the Philippines initially focused on policies to enhance investor protection—raising qualification standards for directors, increasing board committees to monitor performance, and improving disclosure by complying with international financing reporting standards—immediately following the Asian financial crisis. Later, the focus shifted to expanding the investor base by promoting voluntary retirement saving programs. In contrast, after the crisis, the Republic of Korea undertook policies to expand the investor base by eliminating restrictions on investments by foreign investors and simultaneously introducing mutual funds. It improved the market infrastructure by establishing a legal framework for asset-backed securities. And it enhanced investor protection by improving corporate governance practices.

Policies also need to be updated regularly in response to changing market conditions. The Philippines followed earlier pension reforms in 2008 (on voluntary retirement savings) by enacting subsequent policies that established a mandatory pension savings program in 2021. These policies are expected to boost domestic investable savings, potentially contributing further to capital market development.

Policies for capital market development should also be considered within a broader global context. For example, the 2008 global financial crisis was followed by an extended period of low interest rates in high-income countries, leading investors to seek higher yields elsewhere, which increased capital flows into emerging markets. In addition, the European sovereign debt crisis, which began in 2010, weakened the balance sheets of some global banks, forcing them to reduce their presence in low- and middle-income countries. During these periods, firms often shifted from bank lending to capital market financing and, in some cases, moved their funding sources from international to domestic markets (BIS 2018; Cortina, Didier, and Schmukler 2021). The underlying trends driving the recent growth of domestic capital markets broadly reflect these dynamics.

In addition to policy makers, firms can also undertake steps to improve their access to capital market financing.[12] By improving corporate governance and firm disclosure, regardless of local regulatory requirements, firms can attract potential investors. Beyond the measures mentioned above, these steps may include having more independent boards (with stronger outside control), more voting rights for minority shareholders, greater ownership by institutional investors, and less managerial entrenchment. For bond issuances, stronger covenants that restrict issuers from detrimental actions—such as additional debt, large dividend payouts, and divestments of major assets—are important. Investors are especially sensitive to these protections when the issuer is risky, making them particularly relevant for new participants and low- and middle-income countries' firms.

More firm disclosure can be complemented by strong engagement with third-party information providers (such as underwriters, credit rating agencies, and research analysts), which investors often rely on for signals about issuer quality. Firms that engage with such providers tend to have higher capital market financing and lower financing costs (Derrien and Kecskés 2013). For such engagement, choosing local participants over international ones may be preferable, as the former tend to have an information and network advantage—such as first-hand knowledge of local investors, local firms, and the local economy as well as personal relationships with various intermediaries. This approach is especially beneficial for opaque issuances, such as those in markets with limited information flows (most low- and middle-income countries) or firms with limited public information (such as new participants). Furthermore, local stakeholders (such as underwriters and credit rating agencies) may charge firms lower fees for issuing capital due to their lower information-gathering costs.

Capital market development and participation by individual firms can also be supported by international organizations, including multilateral development banks, through the provision of advisory services, issuance of bonds in local currencies, and provision of data on local financial markets. For example, the World Bank Group's Joint Capital Market Program provides technical assistance, often alongside International Finance Corporation transactions in local currency, aimed at delivering a demonstration effect (IFC 2015, 2024).

What Are the Areas for Future Research?

This chapter has discussed potential drivers and policies for capital market growth in low- and middle-income countries. However, it has not undertaken a causal policy analysis necessary to estimate the impact of individual policies. Doing so is challenging because the relationship between such policies and capital market development may not be one-sided, as greater market activity can also induce policy reforms. Moreover, it can be difficult to isolate the impact of individual measures given that multiple reforms are often introduced simultaneously. Further work is needed to uncover such causal impact, especially in low- and middle-income countries, where such evidence can be critical for guiding policy more concretely.

Future work will also benefit from expanding the scope of the analysis in this book. For example, the estimation of real outcomes is restricted to publicly listed firms and thus excludes the majority of firms in an economy. Yet capital market financing could have significant spillover effects for the universe of firms. For example, capital market financing for large corporations might unlock resources for small firms, easing credit constraints. This improved financing might be provided directly through network linkages to issuing firms or indirectly as banks reallocate credit throughout the economy. Understanding the mechanisms and conditions driving these spillovers is important to uncover the true extent of the real effects of developing capital markets.

A natural extension to this book would examine factors that limit firms' growth and, in turn, curb the ability of firms to tap into capital markets. This examination would include barriers in the early stage of the firms' life cycle (such as limited bank credit or lack of private equity), which are not discussed in this book. Relatedly, access to alternative financing sources (such as private capital) may influence firms' decision to participate in public markets.

A key remaining question is whether the presence of institutional investors affects firm participation in capital markets. Given coordination problems in markets, one might expect that firms' decisions to issue would be linked to investors' decisions to invest in markets. They may also affect the type of firms entering markets, as institutional investors can bring substantial advantages over retail investors. Their economies of scale and ability to process information might enable them to diversify risk appropriately, striking a better balance between risk and return and lowering transaction costs (Andrieş, Brodocianu, and Sprincean 2023). It is also important to examine how different types of institutional investors—such as local or foreign, active or passive—affect firm performance and how market frictions constrain investor participation.

Future work could also examine the cost of capital, which is interesting from the perspective of both an issuer and an investor. The cost of capital can determine firm participation in markets and influence how funds are spent after issuance. These effects are expected to differ across types of firms and securities, in addition to being affected by the measures outlined here. From the investor's perspective, examining asset performance in emerging markets can also be valuable. A better understanding of how this performance varies across markets, firms, instruments, financing cycles, and countries can build critical evidence to attract private capital into these markets.

Such work can also expand this book's analysis to include emerging asset classes such as thematic debt. The book only focuses on traditional, noncontingent corporate bonds. In the last decade, there has been a rapid increase in green bonds and other thematic bonds, including in low- and middle-income countries. It would be interesting to examine how these types of bonds are priced relative to conventional instruments, how they are used by issuers in low- and middle-income countries, and what their subsequent effect is on firm outcomes.

Capital markets are an important source of financing for firms, yet significant knowledge gaps remain, especially for low- and middle-income countries. More efforts are needed to address these gaps, some of which are outlined here. By advancing knowledge on these frontiers, public and private stakeholders might be better able to understand the potential of capital market financing and unlock real economic gains.

Notes

1. For a more comprehensive discussion on capital market development policies, refer to Carvajal et al. (2019); World Bank (2020a).

2. This relationship aligns with established economic theory, which suggests that well-functioning capital markets foster economic development. For empirical evidence, refer to Bekaert, Harvey, and Lundblad (2005, 2011) and Wurgler (2000), among many others.

3. Information on pension reforms is from the International Federation of Pension Fund Administrators, a global organization connecting local pension industry associations and fund administrators. During 1990–2022, 30 low- and middle-income countries undertook such pension reforms: Armenia, Belarus, Bolivia, Bulgaria, Colombia, Costa Rica, Croatia, the Dominican Republic, El Salvador, Estonia, Georgia, Ghana, Greece, Hungary, India, Kazakhstan, Latvia, Lithuania, Mexico, Nigeria, Panama, Peru, the Philippines, Poland, Romania, the Russian Federation, the Slovak Republic, Türkiye, Uruguay, and Uzbekistan.

4. The empirical strategy employs a linear panel model with dynamic policy (for example, as in Freyaldenhoven, Hansen, and Shapiro 2019). This approach estimates the impact of pension reforms on CNI by tracking changes relative to the year of reform, beyond what would be expected in a counterfactual drawing on a control group consisting of 117 countries from various income groups that did not implement major pension reforms during the sample period. The model includes country fixed effects to capture time-invariant differences across countries and year fixed effects to capture common shocks or trends experienced by all countries over time. Appendix O provides more details.

5. While this strong demand may result from optimal portfolio allocation or home bias, explicit portfolio limits that favor local securities can also skew some portfolios toward domestic assets (Roldos 2004).

6. Appendix O describes the estimation methodology.

7. For example, an increase of more than 1.5 standard deviations above the mean. Robustness tests with different thresholds were used and yielded similar findings.

8. The sample includes Argentina, Azerbaijan, Bulgaria, Chile, Colombia, Croatia, Georgia, Libya, Mexico, Myanmar, Oman, the Philippines, Russia, Thailand, and Türkiye.

9. A similar analysis plotted the year of the first domestic corporate equity issuance against the first government bond issuance (not shown). The findings reveal that, in many instances, firms can secure equity financing even without a developed sovereign debt market.

10. As a robustness check, an alternative proxy to capture shareholders' rights and role in major corporate decisions (the extent of shareholder rights index from the World Bank's *Doing Business 2020*; World Bank 2020b) is used and found to have similar results (unreported).

11. As a robustness check, an alternative proxy is used to capture disclosure in conflicts of interest between managers and investors (the extent of disclosure index from the World Bank's *Doing Business 2020*; World Bank 2020b), when expropriation risk for investors is particularly high. Results (unreported) are qualitatively similar.

12. Appendix P provides more details about measures that firms can undertake to enhance their access to capital market financing.

References

Abraham, F., J. J. Cortina, and S. L. Schmukler. 2021. "The Rise of Domestic Capital Markets for Corporate Financing: Lessons from East Asia." *Journal of Banking & Finance* 122 (October): 105987. https://doi.org/10.1016/j.jbankfin.2020.105987.

Andrieş, A. M., M. Brodocianu, and N. Sprincean. 2023. "The Role of Institutional Investors in Financial Development." *Economic Change and Restructuring* 56 (1): 345–78.

Bekaert, G., C. R. Harvey, and C. Lundblad. 2005. "Does Financial Liberalization Spur Growth?" *Journal of Financial Economics* 77 (1): 3–55.

Bekaert, G., C. R. Harvey, and C. Lundblad. 2011. "Financial Openness and Productivity." *World Development* 39 (1): 1–19.

BIS (Bank for International Settlements). 2018. "Structural Changes in Banking after the Crisis." CGFS Paper 60, Bank for International Settlements, Basel, Switzerland.

BIS (Bank for International Settlements). 2019. "Establishing Viable Capital Markets." CGFS Paper 62, Bank for International Settlements, Basel, Switzerland.

Boone, A. L., and J. T. White. 2015. "The Effect of Institutional Ownership on Firm Transparency and Information Production." *Journal of Financial Economics* 117 (3): 508–33.

Butler, A. W. 2008. "Distance Still Matters: Evidence from Municipal Bond Underwriting." *Review of Financial Studies* 21 (2): 763–84. https://doi.org/10.1093/rfs/hhn002.

Carvajal, A., R. N. Bebczuk, A. C. Silva, and A. G. Mora. 2019. "Capital Markets Development: Causes, Effects, and Sequencing." Working Paper 148168, World Bank, Washington, DC.

CFA Institute. 2017. *An Assessment of Dual-Class Shares in Brazil: Evidence from Novo Mercado Reform*. Charlottesville, VA: CFA Institute.

Chen, K. C. W., Z. Chen, and K. C. J. Wei. 2009. "Legal Protection of Investors, Corporate Governance, and the Cost of Equity Capital." *Journal of Corporate Finance* 15 (3): 273–89. https://doi.org/10.1016/j.jcorpfin.2009.01.001.

Chen, Y., A. Goyal, and L. Zolotoy. 2022. "Global Board Reforms and the Pricing of IPOs." *Journal of Financial and Quantitative Analysis* 57 (6): 2412–43.

Chinn, M. D., and H. Ito. 2008. "A New Measure of Financial Openness." *Journal of Comparative Policy Analysis* 10 (3): 309–22.

Christensen, H. B., L. Hail, and C. Leuz. 2016. "Capital-Market Effects of Securities Regulation: Prior Conditions, Implementation, and Enforcement." *Review of Financial Studies* 29 (11): 2885–924. https://doi.org/10.1093/rfs/hhw055.

Cortina, J. J., T. Didier, and S. L. Schmukler. 2021. "Global Corporate Debt during Crises: Implications of Switching Borrowing across Markets." *Journal of International Economics* 131 (C): 103487.

Cortina, J. J., M. S. Martinez Peria, S. L. Schmukler, and J. Xiao. 2024. "The Internationalization of China's Equity Markets." *IMF Economic Review* 72: 1–57.

Demekas, D. G., and A. Nerlich. 2020. *Creating Domestic Capital Markets in Developing Countries: Perspectives from Market Participants.* Washington, DC: World Bank.

Derrien, F., and A. Kecskés. 2013. "The Real Effects of Financial Shocks: Evidence from Exogenous Changes in Analyst Coverage." *Journal of Finance* 68 (4): 1407–40. https://doi.org/10.1111/jofi.12042.

Freyaldenhoven, S., C. Hansen, and J. M. Shapiro. 2019. "Pre-event Trends in the Panel Event-study Design." *American Economic Review* 109 (9): 3307–38.

IFC (International Finance Corporation). 2015. *IFC Annual Report 2015: Private Sector Matters for Development.* Washington, DC: World Bank. http://hdl.handle.net/10986/22627.

IFC (International Finance Corporation). 2018. *Corporate Governance Progression Matrix for Listed Companies.* Washington, DC: World Bank.

IFC (International Finance Corporation). 2024. "Joint Capital Markets Program (J-CAP)." Washington, DC: World Bank. https://www.ifc.org/en/what-we-do/sector-expertise /financial-institutions/capital-markets/jcap.

Khurana, I. K., R. Pereira, and X. Martin. 2006. "Firm Growth and Disclosure: An Empirical Analysis." *Journal of Financial and Quantitative Analysis* 41 (2): 357–80.

Klapper, L. F., and I. Love. 2004. "Corporate Governance, Investor Protection, and Performance in Emerging Markets." *Journal of Corporate Finance* 10 (5): 703–28. https://doi.org/10.1016/s0929-1199(03)00046-4.

Lewellen, J., and K. Lewellen. 2022. "Institutional Investors and Corporate Governance: The Incentive to Be Engaged." *Journal of Finance* 77 (1): 213–64.

Lima, B. F., and A. Z. Sanvicente. 2013. "Quality of Corporate Governance and Cost of Equity in Brazil." *Journal of Applied Corporate Finance* 25 (1): 72–80.

Opazo, L., C. Raddatz, and S. L. Schmukler. 2015. "Institutional Investors and Long-Term Investment: Evidence from Chile." *World Bank Economic Review* 29 (3): 479–522.

Packer, F., and E. Remolona. 2012. "Attracting Foreign Participation in Asian Local Currency Bond Markets: The Case of the Asian Bond Fund 2 Initiative." *Pacific Economic Review* 17 (3): 415–33. https://doi.org/10.1111/j.1468-0106.2012.00591.x.

Roldos, M. J. 2004. *Pension Reform, Investment Restrictions, and Capital Markets.* Washington, DC: International Monetary Fund.

Stewart, N. 2010. "Brazilian Companies Blossom on Novo Mercado." *IR Magazine*, February 28, 2010.

World Bank. 2008. *Case Studies in Corporate Governance Reform.* Washington, DC: World Bank.

World Bank. 2020a. *Capital Markets Development: A Primer for Policymakers.* Washington, DC: World Bank.

World Bank. 2020b. *Doing Business 2020.* Washington, DC: World Bank.

Wurgler, J. 2000. "Financial Markets and the Allocation of Capital." *Journal of Financial Economics* 58 (1-2): 187–214.

APPENDIX A

Contribution to the Literature

To date, most of the evidence exploring the role of external finance in enhancing firm growth and aggregate productivity growth focuses primarily on high-income economies.[1] This book addresses this knowledge gap by combining data with extensive coverage both in low- and middle-income countries and in high-income countries on equity and debt issuances and firm balance sheets. It provides an in-depth analysis of how capital market activity shapes capital allocation within and across firms and, more broadly, what contribution capital market development makes to firm performance and productivity growth.

The book analyzes several key aspects of capital market financing, including the use of funds raised in capital markets, the type of firms participating in these markets, and the instruments used in foreign and domestic markets. It contributes to the existing empirical work in each of these areas.

How Do Firms Use Funds Raised in Capital Markets to Finance Firm Growth?

Existing research on how firms use capital markets to fund investment and productive growth is scant, with a notable lack of emphasis on low-income countries. Most of the empirical literature on the use of proceeds examines how firms adjust their capital structure after issuance. For example, firms alter their liabilities, replacing more expensive financing with cheaper funding or changing their debt maturity;[2] in some instances, they accumulate cash and other financial assets (for example, Bruno and Shin 2015; Calomiris, Larrain, and Schmukler 2021; McLean and Zhao 2018). Systematic evidence is more limited on the use of equity and debt markets to increase capital expenditures, investment, and research and development (R&D) activities at the firm level.[3] Didier et al. (2021) examine the link between issuance and firm growth across 65 countries at various income levels. Their research finds that, compared with their counterparts that do not issue, firms that issue equities and bonds grow faster, and the effect is more pronounced among smaller, younger, and high R&D firms. This book adds further depth to this knowledge by showing that more firms in more low- and middle-income countries are using capital markets to finance growth opportunities.

What Type of Firms Are Participating in Capital Markets?

Firms issuing securities in capital markets are typically large, but most literature remains silent about how these firms use the funds to finance growth opportunities compared with smaller firms that also issue (Didier, Levine, and Schmukler 2014; Duffee and Hördahl 2019; Henderson, Jegadeesh, and Weisbach 2006). Among issuers, companies issuing bonds are larger than those relying exclusively on equity finance (Didier, Levine, and Schmukler 2014). Large firms also enjoy more favorable financing terms, issuing bonds with longer maturities and more flexible contracts (OECD 2015). Historically, these large firms tend to capture a disproportionate share of the total value of issuances, especially in low- and middle-income countries (Didier and Schmukler 2013). However, there have been notable regional differences in the past decade, with equity markets in Latin America and the Caribbean and Europe and Central Asia maintaining high levels of concentration, and equity markets in South Asia and East Asia Pacific becoming less concentrated as many new firms have been able to secure equity financing (OECD 2019).[4] Concentration in issuance among large firms could indicate that firms more financially constrained are being excluded from the market.

Market concentration has been associated with less efficient capital allocation, lack of innovation, and slower firm and economic growth (Bae, Bailey, and Kang 2021). In markets where a few firms dominate issuance, new entrants seeking funds for productive activities may struggle to secure financing, hampering their potential for growth. Lack of access to external finance for small or new firms is commonly attributed to frictions linked to information asymmetries. If small firms or those with limited prior issuance face more binding financing constraints, the expectation is that when access to capital market financing alleviates these constraints, there will be a notable increase in firm growth, capital accumulation, and investment. This book addresses a central question: To what extent does capital market inclusion enhance capital allocation and contribute to firm and economic growth in low- and middle-income countries? This book shows that capital markets have allowed smaller, younger, and more financially constrained firms (than those already participating in capital markets) to obtain financing, leading to higher firm performance and economic growth.

What Types of Instruments and Markets Spur Firm Growth?

There is consistent evidence that equity financing, rather than debt, is more appropriate for funding certain innovative activities, motivating further analysis on how access to equity finance may spur firm growth (for example, OECD 2015). Pursuing growth opportunities and participating in innovative activities inherently involves risks and typically requires investments in intangible assets, such as R&D, which have limited collateral value. Equity contracts do not require collateral, and investors directly benefit when the firm succeeds. This helps to explain why young, innovative firms in high-tech industries finance R&D investment almost entirely with internal or external equity (cash flow or public share issues) (Brown, Martinsson, and Peterson 2013). For firms operating in settings with opaque information, highly uncertain investment returns, and insufficient collateral, debt might be a poor substitute for equity financing.[5]

Issuing debt also brings inherent risks. High levels of debt can restrict a firm's ability to pursue new opportunities, as a substantial portion of earnings is used to repay existing debt. This limitation reduces flexibility, hindering innovation and expansion.[6] Indeed, the expansion of corporate debt in low- and middle-income countries after the global financial crisis highlights that, as firms issued more bonds, their leverage positions rose, and their financial performance worsened (Abraham, Cortina, and Schmukler 2021; Alfaro et al. 2019). This book shows that both equity and debt financing in capital markets lead to improved firm performance, indicating that these markets are able to ease financial constraints, although equity finance displays the strongest correlation with firm growth.

Issuing securities in domestic or foreign markets can offer different advantages. Identifying how firms use these markets to finance investments can deepen understanding of their impact on firm growth. Existing literature highlights several advantages of engaging in offshore markets, such as accessing a broader base of investors, securing improved financing terms and less expensive capital, and facilitating currency hedging and enhanced risk management.[7] Despite these benefits, high fixed costs and information frictions often preclude small firms from participating in international markets (Calomiris et al. 2022; Gozzi et al. 2015; Lang, Raedy, and Yetman 2003). Less explored is how firms that do access these markets use the proceeds. To what extent do firms raise funds in international markets to accumulate capital and undertake investments? Are such decisions different from raising funds domestically?[8] This book documents extensive issuance in both foreign and domestic markets. However, small, more financially constrained firms, which have greater access to domestic markets, tend to experience the largest gains in performance. So, issuance activity in domestic markets is strongly correlated with larger gains in aggregate productivity.

How Has This Book Expanded the Institutional Knowledge on Capital Market Development?

This book builds on and contributes to the existing body of institutional knowledge on capital market development. Much of the recent analytical work has focused on identifying the key factors and conditions needed to foster capital market growth. For example, the World Bank's Joint Capital Market Program has produced several reports that synthesize the existing literature, survey private sector participants, and translate findings into actionable policy insights (Carvajal et al. 2019; Demekas and Nerlich 2020; World Bank 2020). Other publications have also examined these important issues (De la Torre, Ize, and Schmukler 2012; Didier and Schmukler 2013; Feyen et al. 2015; IMF and World Bank 2015, 2018, 2021; World Bank 2017). The emphasis on studying the factors that lead to well-functioning capital markets is understandable given their close alignment with policy objectives. Equally important for the capital market development agenda, however, is the need to advance understanding of the link between capital markets, the financing of firms, and the real economy, which this book undertakes.

This book complements a recent World Bank publication, *Unleashing Productivity through Firm Financing* (Didier and Cusolito 2024). While that book focuses mostly on private firms in a select sample of high- and middle-income countries, it does examine the link between overall firm financing and the real economy. The current book extends and expands this literature by focusing exclusively on capital market financing in emerging markets and developing economies, including low-income countries. Doing so allows for a richer analysis of the impacts on productivity (by going beyond fund allocation), exploring heterogeneous effects along dimensions of relevance to capital markets and expanding the country sample to improve the coverage of more low-income countries. And more important, such an extension also highlights the expansion of capital markets to more countries, sectors, and firms.

Finally, this book complements a series of recent publications by other international organizations that explore the role and significance of capital markets. Collectively, these publications reveal the recent progress in low- and middle-income countries compared with their higher-income counterparts, while also highlighting persistent gaps (CGFS 2019). Some books focus on specific aspects of capital markets, such as recent developments in corporate governance (OECD 2021) or new financing instruments for micro, small, and medium firms (IDB 2023). These works offer broad yet crucial policy recommendations, including the need to strengthen regulatory and legal frameworks and broaden the base of investors. Aligned with these discussions, this book precisely identifies the firms and circumstances where access to capital markets fosters growth most effectively. It provides insights into the potential for developing capital markets and estimates their impact by capturing the nuances of different types of firms.

Notes

1. For example, Gopinath et al. (2017) study a group of high-income countries in Europe. Two exceptions are Arellano, Bai, and Zhang (2012) and Bau and Matray (2023). Arellano, Bai, and Zhang (2012) study the impact of financial market development on a sample of 27 European countries at different income levels. As a natural experiment, Bau and Matray (2023) examine the impact of capital liberalization on capital allocation and productivity at the industry level in India.

2. Using a sample of Italian firms, the seminal work from Pagano, Panetta, and Zingales (1998) shows that many companies issue equity not to finance future investments, but to rebalance their accounts after they have made large investments. Other work shows that, instead of being motivated by investment opportunities, firms time their issuance to take advantage of high market valuations (Baker and Wurgler 2002; Graham and Harvey 2001; Hertzel and Li 2010). Refer to Graham and Leary (2011) for a review of the empirical literature on capital structure.

3. There are exceptions, but existing studies focus either on a specific set of securities or on individual countries. For example, Kim and Weisbach (2008) examine the use of funds on capital expenditures and R&D from equity issuances in a sample of 38 countries. Rahaman (2011) examines the role of equity and debt financing on firm growth for firms in Ireland and the United Kingdom. Cortina et al. (2024) examine firm growth from access to equity finance in China.

4. The literature typically uses the share of market capitalization from the largest 5 (or 10) companies as a measure of market concentration. Abraham, Cortina, and Schmukler (2021) provide similar evidence comparing the corporate bond markets in Latin America and East Asia.

5. Whereas firms that hold more tangible assets appear to be more likely to issue new corporate bonds (Davis, Maslar, and Roseman 2017), firms that invest in more intangible assets may be more likely to issue stock (Hosono and Takizawa 2017).

6. The debt overhang concept was first analyzed by Myers (1977) and later studied extensively in the corporate finance literature (for example, Leland 1998; Manso 2008).

7. Borrowers also benefit from greater liquidity and diversification when tapping into more "complete" offshore markets (Black and Munro 2010). Feyen et al. (2015) claim that the increase in external bond issuance in emerging markets and low- and middle-income economies in the period following the global financial crisis was driven by global push factors—that is, loose financial conditions that made external issuance more attractive due to lower financing costs. There is also evidence that international bonds have longer maturities (Black and Munro 2010; Cortina, Didier, and Schmukler 2018a, 2018b). And by substituting domestic for foreign financing, firms might be able to withstand negative shocks to the domestic economy that affect the supply of capital—that is, they diversify their funding sources (Cortina, Didier, and Schmukler 2021).

8. One exception is Gozzi, Levine, and Schmukler (2010). Studying firm performance following debt and equity issuances in international markets, they find that both markets have similar effects on firm performance. Most of the empirical literature typically focuses on liberalization episodes to examine the potential benefit to domestic firms. The evidence suggests that liberalization typically lowers the cost of capital (Chari and Henry 2004, 2008). The evidence on the impact of liberalization on firm growth is more mixed, with some studies finding a positive impact (Bekaert, Harvey, and Lundblad 2005, 2011; Gupta and Yuan 2009; Quinn and Toyoda 2008) and others finding negative effects (Edison and Warnock 2008; Kose et al. 2009; McLean, Pontiff, and Zhao 2022; Prasad, Rogoff, and Kose 2003).

References

Abraham, F., J. J. Cortina, and S. L. Schmukler. 2021. "The Rise of Domestic Capital Markets for Corporate Financing: Lessons from East Asia." *Journal of Banking & Finance* 122 (October): 105987. https://doi.org/10.1016/j.jbankfin.2020.105987.

Alfaro, L., G. Asis, A. Chari, and U. Panizza. 2019. "Corporate Debt, Firm Size, and Financial Fragility in Emerging Markets." *Journal of International Economics* 118 (May): 1–19. https://doi.org/10.1016/j.jinteco.2019.01.002.

Arellano, C., Y. Bai, and J. Zhang. 2012. "Firm Dynamics and Financial Development." *Journal of Monetary Economics* 59 (6): 533–49. https://doi.org/10.1016/j.jmoneco.2012.06.006.

Bae, K.-H., W. Bailey, and J. Kang. 2021. "Why Is Stock Market Concentration Bad for the Economy?" *Journal of Financial Economics* 140 (2): 436–59. https://doi.org/10.1016/j.jfineco.2021.01.002.

Baker, M., and J. Wurgler. 2002. "Market Timing and Capital Structure." *Journal of Finance* 57 (1): 1–32. https://doi.org/10.1111/1540-6261.00414.

Bau, N., and A. Matray. 2023. "Misallocation and Capital Market Integration: Evidence from India." *Econometrica* 91 (1): 67–106. https://doi.org/10.3982/ECTA19039.

Bekaert, G., C. Harvey, and C. Lundblad. 2005. "Does Financial Liberalization Spur Growth?" *Journal of Financial Economics* 77 (1): 3–55. https://doi.org/10.1016/j.jfineco.2004.05.007.

Bekaert, G., C. R. Harvey, and C. Lundblad. 2011. "Financial Openness and Productivity." *World Development* 39 (1): 1–19. https://doi.org/10.1016/j.worlddev.2010.06.016.

Black, S., and A. E. Munro. 2010. "Why Issue Bonds Offshore?" Working Paper 52, Bank for International Settlements, Basel, Switzerland. https://doi.org/10.2139/ssrn.1725989.

Brown, J. R., G. Martinsson, and B. C. Peterson. 2013. "Law, Stock Markets, and Innovation." *Journal of Finance* 68 (4): 1517–49. https://doi.org/10.1111/jofi.12040.

Bruno, V., and H. S. Shin. 2015. "Capital Flows and the Risk-Taking Channel of Monetary Policy." *Journal of Monetary Economics* 71 (April): 119–32. https://doi.org/10.1016/j.jmoneco.2014.11.011.

Calomiris, C. W., M. Larrain, and S. L. Schmukler. 2021. "Capital Inflows, Equity Issuance Activity, and Corporate Investment." *Journal of Financial Intermediation* 46 (April). https://doi.org/10.1016/j.jfi.2019.100845.

Calomiris, C. W., M. Larrain, S. L. Schmukler, and T. Williams. 2022. "Large International Corporate Bonds: Investor Behavior and Firm Responses." *Journal of International Economics* 137 (April): 103624. https://doi.org/10.1016/j.jinteco.2022.103624.

Carvajal, A. F., R. N. Bebczuk, A. C. Silva, and A. G. Mora. 2019. *Capital Markets Development: Causes, Effects, and Sequencing.* Washington, DC: World Bank. https://documents.worldbank.org/en/publication/documents-reports/documentdetail/701021588343376548/capital-markets-development-causes-effects-and-sequencing.

CGFS (Committee on the Global Financial System). 2019. "Establishing Viable Capital Markets." CGFS Papers 62, Bank for International Settlements, Basel, Switzerland. https://www.bis.org/publ/cgfs62.pdf.

Chari, A., and P. B. Henry. 2004. "Risk Sharing and Asset Prices: Evidence from a Natural Experiment." *Journal of Finance* 59 (3): 1295–324. https://doi.org/10.1111/j.1540-6261.2004.00663.x.

Chari, A., and P. B. Henry. 2008. "Firm-Specific Information and the Efficiency of Investment." *Journal of Financial Economics* 87 (3): 636–55. https://doi.org/10.1016/j.jfineco.2007.03.008.

Cortina, J. J., T. Didier, and S. L. Schmukler. 2018a. "Corporate Debt Maturity in Developing Countries: Sources of Long and Short-Termism." *The World Economy* 41 (12): 3288–316. https://doi.org/10.1111/twec.12632.

Cortina, J. J., T. Didier, and S. L. Schmukler. 2018b. "Corporate Borrowing and Debt Maturity: The Effects of Market Access and Crises." Washington, DC: World Bank. https://doi.org/10.1596/1813-9450-7815.

Cortina, J. J., T. Didier, and S. L. Schmukler. 2021. "Global Corporate Debt during Crises: Implications of Switching Borrowing across Markets." *Journal of International Economics* 131 (July): 103487. https://doi.org/10.1016/j.jinteco.2021.103487.

Cortina, J. J., M. S. Martinez Peria, S. L. Schmukler, and J. Xiao. 2024. "The Internationalization of China's Equity Markets." *IMF Economic Review* (2024): 1–57.

Davis, R. L., D. A. Maslar, and B. S. Roseman. 2017. "Secondary Market Trading and the Cost of New Debt Issuance." *SSRN Electronic Journal*. https://doi.org/10.2139/ssrn.2954857.

De la Torre, A., A. Ize, and S. L. Schmukler. 2012. "Financial Development in Latin America and the Caribbean: The Road Ahead [El desarrollo financiero en América Latina y el Caribe: El camino por delante]." Washington, DC: World Bank.

Demekas, D. G., and A. Nerlich. 2020. *Creating Domestic Capital Markets in Developing Countries: Perspectives from Market Participants*. Washington, DC: International Finance Corporation. https://doi.org/10.1596/33617.

Didier, T., and A. Cusolito. 2024. *Unleashing Productivity through Firm Financing*. Washington, DC: World Bank. http://hdl.handle.net/10986/42194.

Didier, T., R. Levine, R. L. Montanes, and S. L. Schmukler. 2021. "Capital Market Financing and Firm Growth." *Journal of International Money and Finance* 118 (July): 102459. https://doi.org/10.1016/j.jimonfin.2021.102459.

Didier, T., R. Levine, and S. L. Schmukler. 2014. "Capital Market Financing, Firm Growth, Firm Size Distribution." Working Paper 20336, National Bureau of Economic Research, Cambridge, MA. https://doi.org/10.3386/w20336.

Didier, T., and S. L. Schmukler. 2013. "The Financing and Growth of Firms in China and India: Evidence from Capital Markets." *Journal of International Money and Finance* 39 (December): 111–37. https://doi.org/10.1016/j.jimonfin.2013.06.021.

Duffee, G., and P. Hördahl. 2019. "Corporate Bond Use in Asia and the United States." Working Paper 102, Bank for International Settlements, Basel, Switzerland.

Edison, H. J., and F. E. Warnock. 2008. "Cross-Border Listings, Capital Controls, and Equity Flows to Emerging Markets." *Journal of International Money and Finance* 27 (6): 1013–27. https://doi.org/10.1016/j.jimonfin.2008.05.001.

Feyen, E., S. Ghosh, K. Kibuuka, and S. Farazi. 2015. "Global Liquidity and External Bond Issuance in Emerging Markets and Developing Economies." Policy Research Working Paper 7363, World Bank, Washington, DC. https://doi.org/10.1596/1813-9450-7363.

Gopinath, G., Ş. Kalemli-Özcan, L. Karabarbounis, and C. Villegas-Sanchez. 2017. "Capital Allocation and Productivity in South Europe." *Quarterly Journal of Economics* 132 (4): 1915–67. https://doi.org/10.1093/qje/qjx024.

Gozzi, J. C., R. Levine, M. S. Martinez Peria, and S. L. Schmukler. 2015. "How Firms Use Corporate Bond Markets under Financial Globalization." *Journal of Banking & Finance* 58 (September): 532–51. https://doi.org/10.1016/j.jbankfin.2015.03.017.

Gozzi, J. C., R. Levine, and S. L. Schmukler. 2010. "Patterns of International Capital Raisings." *Journal of International Economics* 80 (1): 45–57. https://doi.org/10.1016/j.jinteco.2009.05.007.

Graham, J. R., and C. R. Harvey. 2001. "The Theory and Practice of Corporate Finance: Evidence from the Field." *Journal of Financial Economics* 60 (2–3): 187–243. https://doi.org/10.1016/s0304-405x(01)00044-7.

Graham, J., and M. Leary. 2011. "A Review of Empirical Capital Structure Research and Directions for the Future." *Annual Review of Financial Economics* 3 (2011): 309–45. https://doi.org/10.1146/annurev-financial-102710-144821.

Gupta, N., and K. Yuan. 2009. "On the Growth Effect of Stock Market Liberalizations." *Review of Financial Studies* 22 (11): 4715–52. https://doi.org/10.1093/rfs/hhp001.

Henderson, B. J., N. Jegadeesh, and M. S. Weisbach. 2006. "World Markets for Raising New Capital." *Journal of Financial Economics* 82 (1): 63–101. https://doi.org/10.1016/j.jfineco.2005.08.004.

Hertzel, M. G., and Z. Li. 2010. "Behavioral and Rational Explanations of Stock Price Performance around SEOs: Evidence from a Decomposition of Market-To-Book Ratios." *Journal of Financial and Quantitative Analysis* 45 (4): 935–58. https://doi.org/10.1017/s002210901000030x.

Hosono, K., and M. Takizawa. 2017. "Intangible Capital and the Choice of External Financing Sources." Discussion Paper 17080, Research Institute of Economy, Trade and Industry (RIETI), Tokyo. *RePEc: Research Papers in Economics* (May).

IDB (Inter-American Development Bank). 2023. *The Role of Capital Markets in Funding MSMEs in Latin America and the Caribbean.* Washington, DC: Inter-American Development Bank.

IMF (International Monetary Fund) and World Bank. 2015. "From Billions to Trillions: Transforming Development Finance." Joint Development Committee Discussion Note, World Bank Group, Washington, DC.

IMF (International Monetary Fund) and World Bank. 2018. "Recent Developments on Local Currency Bond Markets in Emerging Economies." Staff Note for the G-20 International Financial Architecture Working Group (IFAWGC), Washington, DC.

IMF (International Monetary Fund) and World Bank. 2021. "Guidance Note for Developing Government Local Currency Bond Markets." IMF Analytical Note 2021/001, Washington, DC.

Kim, W., and M. Weisbach. 2008. "Motivations for Public Equity Offers: An International Perspective." *Journal of Financial Economics* 87 (2): 281–307. https://doi.org/10.1016/j.jfineco.2006.09.010.

Kose, M. A., E. S. Prasad, K. S. Rogoff, and S.-J. Wei. 2009. "Financial Globalization and Economic Policies." *IMF Staff Papers* 56 (1): 8–62.

Lang, M., J. S. Raedy, and M. H. Yetman. 2003. "How Representative Are Firms That Are Cross-Listed in the United States? An Analysis of Accounting Quality." *Journal of Accounting Research* 41 (2): 363–86. https://doi.org/10.1111/1475-679x.00108.

Leland, H. E. 1998. "Agency Costs, Risk Management, and Capital Structure." *Journal of Finance* 53 (4): 1213–43. https://doi.org/10.1111/0022-1082.00051.

Manso, G. 2008. "Investment Reversibility and Agency Cost of Debt." *Econometrica* 76 (2): 437–42. https://doi.org/10.1111/j.1468-0262.2008.00838.x.

McLean, R. D., J. Pontiff, and M. Zhao. 2022. "A Closer Look at the Effects of Equity Market Liberalization in Emerging Markets." *Review of Corporate Finance Studies* 13 (3): 858–87. https://doi.org/10.1093/rcfs/cfac023.

McLean, R. D., and M. Zhao. 2018. "Cash Savings and Capital Markets." *Journal of Empirical Finance* 47 (June): 49–64. https://doi.org/10.1016/j.jempfin.2018.02.001.

Myers, S. C. 1977. "Determinants of Corporate Borrowing." *Journal of Financial Economics* 5 (2): 147–75.

OECD (Organisation for Economic Co-operation and Development). 2015. *Growth Companies, Access to Capital Markets, and Corporate Governance.* Paris: OECD Publishing. https://www.oecd.org/g20/topics/framework-strong-sustainable-balanced -growth/OECD-Growth-Companies-Access-to-Capital-Markets-and-Corporate -Governance.pdf.

OECD (Organisation for Economic Co-operation and Development). 2019. *Equity Market Development in Latin America: Enhancing Access to Corporate Finance.* Paris: OECD Publishing. https://www.oecd.org/corporate/ca/Latin-American-Equity -Markets-2019.pdf.

OECD (Organisation for Economic Co-operation and Development). 2021. *The Future of Corporate Governance in Capital Markets Following the COVID-19 Crisis, Corporate Governance.* Paris: OECD Publishing. https://doi.org/10.1787/efb2013c-en.

Pagano, M., F. Panetta, and L. Zingales. 1998. "Why Do Companies Go Public? An Empirical Analysis." *Journal of Finance* 53 (1): 27–64. https://doi.org /10.1111/0022-1082.25448.

Prasad, E., S. Rogoff, and A. Kose. 2003. "Effects of Financial Globalization on Developing Countries: Some Empirical Evidence." IMF Occasional Paper 220 (December), International Monetary Fund, Washington, DC. https://doi.org /10.5089/9781498329835.007.

Quinn, D. P., and A. M. Toyoda. 2008. "Does Capital Account Liberalization Lead to Growth?" *Review of Financial Studies* 21 (3): 1403–49. https://doi.org/10.1093/rfs /hhn034.

Rahaman, M. M. 2011. "Access to Financing and Firm Growth." *Journal of Banking & Finance* 35 (3): 709–23. https://doi.org/10.1016/j.jbankfin.2010.09.005.

World Bank. 2017. *Promoting the Use of Capital Markets for Infrastructure Financing: Lessons for Securities Markets Regulators in Emerging Market Economies.* Washington, DC: World Bank.

World Bank. 2020. *Capital Markets Development: A Primer for Policymakers.* Washington, DC: World Bank.

APPENDIX B

Country and Economy Income Classifications

To ensure that the number of countries in each group stays constant over time, this book adopts a static definition of low-, middle-, and high-income countries based on the World Bank's income group classifications from 1990.[1] Changing the classifications would complicate the analysis since changes could obscure whether trends were due to more countries entering capital markets or to changes in countries' income status. Since the aim is to determine whether countries initially categorized as low- and middle-income countries, which had little to no access to capital markets, were eventually able to gain access to capital markets, 1990 was chosen as the year for classifying countries by income group.

The World Bank assigns countries to income groups based on gross national income (GNI) per capita, expressed in US dollars. In 1990, the thresholds were

- Low-income: ≤ US$610

- Middle-income: US$611–US$7,620

- High-income: > US$7,620.

To keep income classification thresholds fixed in real terms, the thresholds are adjusted annually for inflation by the World Bank using the Special Drawing Rights (SDR) deflator, a weighted average of the gross domestic product (GDP) deflators of China, Japan, the United Kingdom, the United States, and the euro area. In total, there are 106 low- and middle-income countries, China, and 40 high-income countries (table B.1).[2]

TABLE B.1

Countries, Economies, Special Regions, and Territories Examined in the Book

High-income	Middle-income	Middle-income *cont.*	Low-income
Aruba	Algeria	Macao SAR, China	Bangladesh
Australia	Angola	Malaysia	Cambodia
Austria	Argentina	Malta	China
Bahamas, The	Azerbaijan	Marshall Islands	Egypt,
Belgium	Bahrain	Mauritius	Arab Rep.
Bermuda	Barbados	Mexico	Equatorial
British Virgin Islands	Belarus	Micronesia, Fed. Sts.	Guinea
Canada	Bolivia	Mongolia	Ghana
Cayman Islands	Bosnia and	Montenegro	India
Cyprus	Herzegovina	Morocco	Indonesia
Denmark	Botswana	Nicaragua	Kenya
Faroe Islands	Brazil	Oman	Lao PDR
Finland	Bulgaria	Panama	Liberia
France	Chile	Papua New Guinea	Madagascar
Germany	Colombia	Paraguay	Malawi
Greenland	Costa Rica	Peru	Maldives
Hong Kong SAR, China	Côte d'Ivoire	Philippines	Mozambique
Iceland	Croatia	Poland	Myanmar
Ireland	Czechia	Portugal	Nepal
Israel	Dominican Republic	Puerto Rico (US)	Nigeria
Italy	Ecuador	Romania	Pakistan
Japan	El Salvador	Russian Federation	Rwanda
Kuwait	Estonia	Saudi Arabia	Sierra Leone
Liechtenstein	Fiji	Senegal	Sri Lanka
Luxembourg	Georgia	Serbia	Sudan
Monaco	Gibraltar (UK)	Slovak Republic	Tanzania
Netherlands	Greece	Slovenia	Togo
New Zealand	Guam	South Africa	Uganda
Norway	Guatemala	Syrian Arab Republic	Viet Nam
Qatar	Hungary	Thailand	Zambia
Singapore	Iran, Islamic Rep.	Trinidad and Tobago	
Spain	Iraq	Tunisia	
Sweden	Isle of Man	Türkiye	
Switzerland	Jamaica	Ukraine	
Taiwan, China	Jordan	Uruguay	
Turks and Caicos	Kazakhstan	Uzbekistan	
Islands (UK)	Kiribati	Venezuela, RB	
United Arab Emirates	Korea, Rep.	Zimbabwe	
United Kingdom	Latvia		
United States	Lebanon		
United States Virgin	Libya		
Islands	Lithuania		

Source: The classification year of countries into income groups is 1990 using the World Bank income categories.

Note: This table presents the countries, economies, special regions, and territories included in this book. Because of its large size and shift from low-income to upper-middle-income status during the sample period, China is excluded from both low-income and middle-income categories and is presented separately throughout the book.

Notes

1. Country classifications have evolved over time, including countries that play significant roles in today's global economy. For example, China was a low-income country in 1990 but is now an upper-middle-income country. For this book, the aim is to find whether countries classified as low- and middle-income at the beginning of the period were able to access capital markets eventually and grow.

2. Even though China is classified as a low-income country based on the World Bank's classification in 1990, because of its large size and its transition from low-income to upper-middle-income status during the sample period, it is presented separately and excluded from both low-income and middle-income categories.

APPENDIX C

Data

The Securities Data Company Platinum database from LSEG, a comprehensive data set on new bond issues, mergers and acquisitions, syndicated loans, and equity, is the main database used in chapter 2 and other chapters. This book uses data on the universe of equity and bond issuances for publicly listed and privately held companies. While data for issuances in the United States start in the 1970s, coverage of other markets starts later, with most regional databases starting in 1990. For this reason, the sample is restricted to 1990–2022. The Securities Data Company Platinum database is updated continually, meaning that any initially missed capital issuances are added in subsequent updates. Since Securities Data Company Platinum provides the date of each issuance, there is no lag in including new firms accessing capital markets, even if their issuance is added later. The countries included are presented in table B.1 in appendix B. The Securities Data Company Platinum database provides detailed transaction-level information and offers comprehensive coverage of worldwide bond and equity issuances, which helps to document and characterize capital markets around the world.[1] This granularity of the data enables detailed insights into the participation of firms and countries.

The data set has certain limitations, including the lack of information on whether firms default on their bond debt and whether callable bonds are bought back. Despite these gaps, data coverage appears to be strong (figure C.1). Issuance-level data on bond issuances from the Securities Data Company Platinum database are aggregated and compared with similarly aggregated data from the World Bank Global Financial Development Database (GFDD), which uses Dealogic data. In addition, cumulative net bond issuance is calculated by aggregating individual bond issuances from the Securities Data Company Platinum database globally, assuming full repayment at maturity for each security, and this series is compared with data from the Bank for International Settlements (BIS) Debt Securities Statistics. The results indicate that the coverage of the Securities Data Company Platinum database is quite similar to that of Dealogic and the BIS, both with regard to levels and time variation.

FIGURE C.1

The Securities Data Company Platinum from LSEG Provides
Accurate Data for Corporate Bond Markets from 2000 to 2022

2020 US$, billions   **2020 US$, billions**

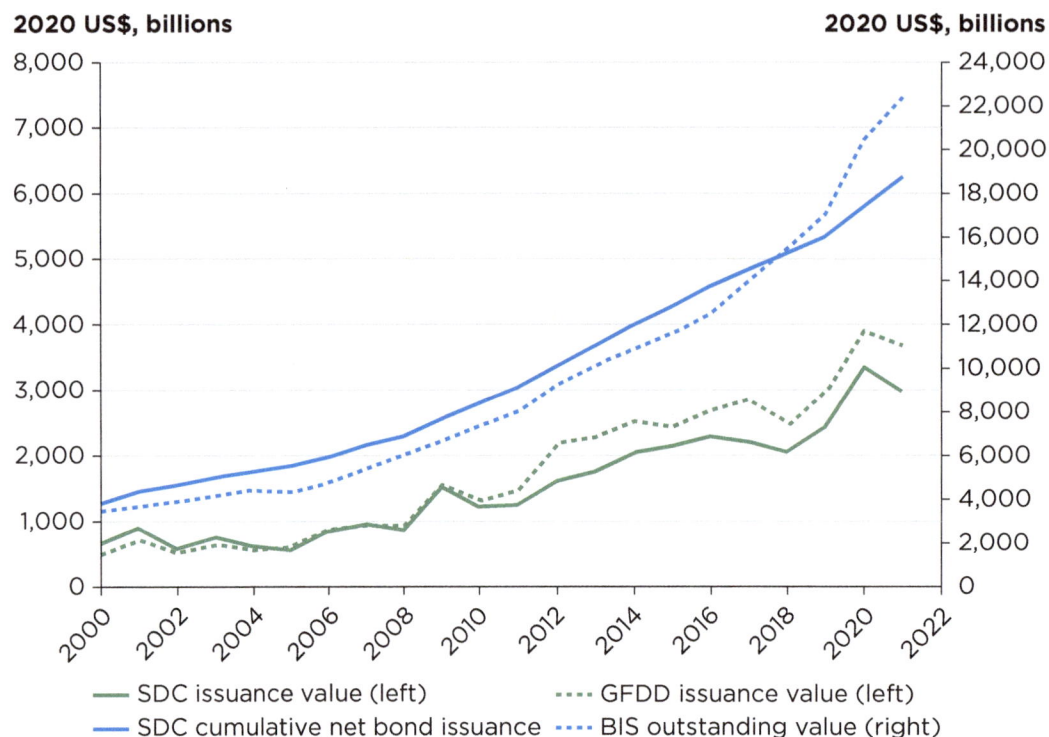

— SDC issuance value (left)   ···· GFDD issuance value (left)
— SDC cumulative net bond issuance   ···· BIS outstanding value (right)

Source: Calculations using issuance data from the Securities Data Company Platinum
database from LSEG and the World Bank Global Financial Development Database and
securities data from the Bank of International Settlements Debt Securities Statistics.
Note: This figure compares the coverage of the LSEG's Securities Data Company
Platinum database data with that of other databases on nonfinancial corporate bonds.
The global issuance value of bonds annually is compared with that reported by the
World Bank GFDD. In addition, the global CNBI, calculated from the bond issuance data,
assuming full repayment of bonds at maturity, is compared with figures reported by the
BIS Debt Securities Statistics. CNBI for year *Y* is computed as the sum of bond issuance
(minus bonds that matured) between 1990 and year *Y*. The volume of issuance and the
CNBI include both domestic and international issuances by nonfinancial firms in each
country. All data are expressed in billions of 2020 US dollars. BIS = Bank for International
Settlements; CNBI = cumulative net bond issuance; GFDD = Global Financial
Development Database; SDC = Securities Data Company Platinum.

This book concentrates on nonfinancial firms.[2] For this reason, finance, insurance, and real estate[3] are removed from the data set.[4] Government issuances are also removed—issuances by national, local, and regional governments—as well as issuances of government agencies and regional agencies. State-owned enterprises (SOEs), defined according to the International Monetary Fund criterion of firms with direct state ownership of 50 percent or more, are included (SOEs are expected to account for a minority of issuances).[5] Issuances by supranationals such as the International Finance Corporation and the World Bank are also removed. Types of issuances, such as asset-backed, mortgage-backed, and financial credit agency issuances are also excluded.

To compare issuance amounts across decades, nominal issuance is converted to constant 2020 US dollars, using the 2020 US consumer price index from the US Bureau of Labor Statistics. To compare issuance amounts across countries, issuance is taken as a percentage of country gross domestic product (GDP), using the World Bank's World Development Indicators database, which is also used for data on domestic credit to the private sector by banks.

Notes

1. The Securities Data Company Platinum database provides issuance characteristics such as issuer name, date of issue, market of issue, amount issued, country of issuer, as well as many others.
2. Nonfinancial firms are firms with a Standard Industrial Classification (SIC) code between 0 and 5,999 and between 6,800 and 9,099.
3. Finance, insurance, and real estate firms are firms with an SIC code between 6,000 and 6,800.
4. Figure 1.1 in chapter 1 includes both nonfinancial and financial firms. Appendix D reviews financial firm issuance and compares it to nonfinancial firm issuance.
5. The data in this book include SOEs but do not allow for their identification. Hernando-Kaminsky (2024) documents that, on average, SOEs accounted for 17 percent of total annual gross bond issuance in advanced economies and 18 percent in developing economies during the 1991–2020 period. These statistics are based on a subset of 31 advanced economies and 34 developing economies. In equity markets, between 1990 and 2009, SOE listings represented, on average, 23 percent of all public offerings per year for a subset of emerging and developing economies (World Bank 2021). Additionally, there is evidence to suggest that SOE listings encourage nongovernment-owned companies to list during the early phases of market development (World Bank 2021).

References

Hernando-Kaminsky, P. 2024. "Crowding Out and Banking Crises." Unpublished manuscript, International Finance Corporation, Washington, DC.

World Bank. 2021. *Listing State-Owned Enterprises in Emerging and Developing Economies: Lessons Learned from 30 Years of Success and Failure.* Washington, DC: World Bank.

APPENDIX D

Financial Firms

While this book focuses primarily on the growth of capital markets for nonfinancial firms, capital markets for financial firms have also grown during the past three decades, with cumulative net capital issuance (CNI) reaching approximately US$30 trillion in 2022. These firms account for a significant portion of total CNI. This appendix takes a closer look at these firms and how their issuance compares with the issuance of nonfinancial firms. A firm is classified as financial if its Standard Industrial Classification (SIC) code is between 6,000 and 6,999. Specifically, the firms that have an SIC code between these intervals are firms operating primarily in finance, insurance, and real estate.

Throughout most of the sample period, nonfinancial firms have had more CNI than financial firms, with their share hovering around 53 percent (figure D.1, panel a). However, in some surges, financial firms have issued more capital, causing their share to rise. The first surge occurred in 1990–99, and the second occurred in the lead-up to the global financial crisis. During the first surge, the share of total CNI held by financial firms reached only 49 percent, and in the period leading up to the global financial crisis, the share of CNI held by financial firms surpassed that held by nonfinancial firms, with financial firms accounting for 52 percent of total CNI in 2008. After this period, the share held by financial firms fell and stabilized at about 46 percent.

A general pattern for both types of firms is the reliance on new bond debt (figure D.1, panel b). However, the difference between new bond debt issuance and new equity issuance is notably larger for financial firms than for nonfinancial firms: financial firms issued approximately 7 times more bond debt than equity, whereas nonfinancial firms issued between 2 and 3.5 times more bond debt than equity. While the bond-to-equity issuance ratio remained relatively stable over time for financial firms, it increased steadily for nonfinancial firms. In 1990–99, nonfinancial firms issued 2 times more bond debt than equity, and in 2010–22, they issued around 3.5 times more bond debt than equity.

FIGURE D.1

Financial Firms Have Typically Held a Minority Share of CNI, Depending Heavily on New Bond Debt

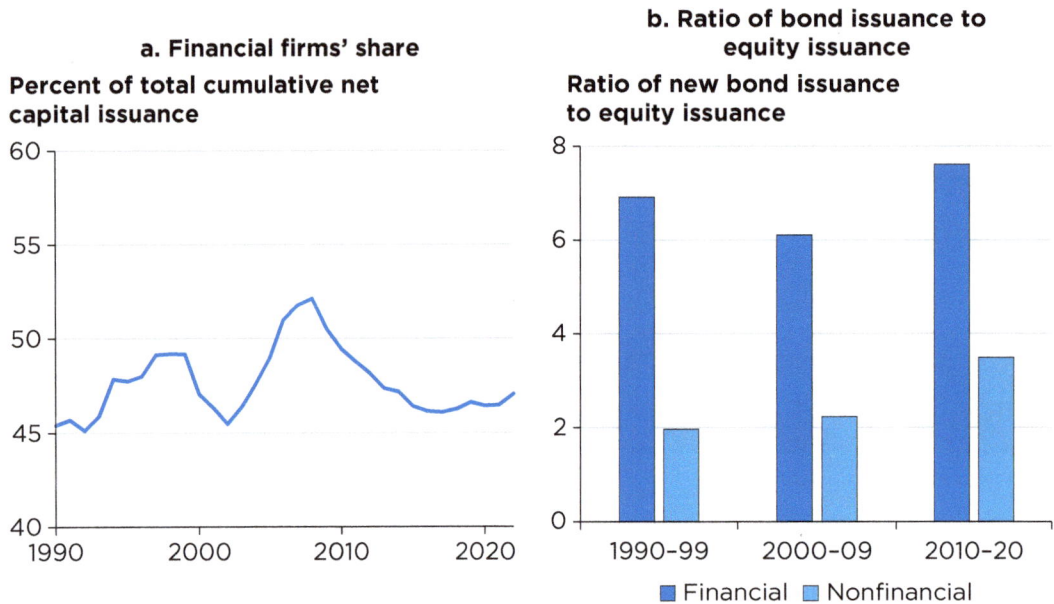

a. Financial firms' share

Percent of total cumulative net capital issuance

b. Ratio of bond issuance to equity issuance

Ratio of new bond issuance to equity issuance

■ Financial ■ Nonfinancial

Source: Calculations using issuance data from the Securities Data Company Platinum database from LSEG.

Note: This figure compares the amount of CNI as well as the ratio of new bond issuance and equity issuance for financial and nonfinancial firms. Panel a presents the financial firms' annual share of the total amount of CNI. CNI for year *Y* is computed as the sum of equity issuance and bond issuance (minus bonds that matured) between 1990 and year *Y*. Panel b presents the ratio between the average amount of new bond and new equity issuance for each of the past three decades for financial and nonfinancial firms. CNI = cumulative net capital issuance.

APPENDIX E

Global Market Capitalization Before 1990

The primary data used in this book are new capital issuances for 1990–2022. The reason for not extending the sample back further stems from the limited availability of data. Therefore, the figures in this book depict capital markets as commencing in 1990, even though capital markets predate this period. While initially relatively small at the beginning of the 1980s,[1] world market capitalization accelerated notably around the mid-1980s, with stock market capitalization surging to around US$19 trillion by 1990 (figure E.1).[2] In emerging markets, stock market capitalization followed a similar pattern, although the values are just a fraction of world market capitalization.

Since the available pre-1990 data are aggregated at the country level, they do not allow for firm-level analysis, so other data sources are used. For this book, the main indicator of capital market activity is cumulative net capital issuance, which is calculated each year as the sum of equity and bond issuances since 1990 minus bonds that have matured since 1990. The level before 1990 is normalized to zero.

FIGURE E.1

Global Stock Market Capitalization Grew in the 1980–90 Period

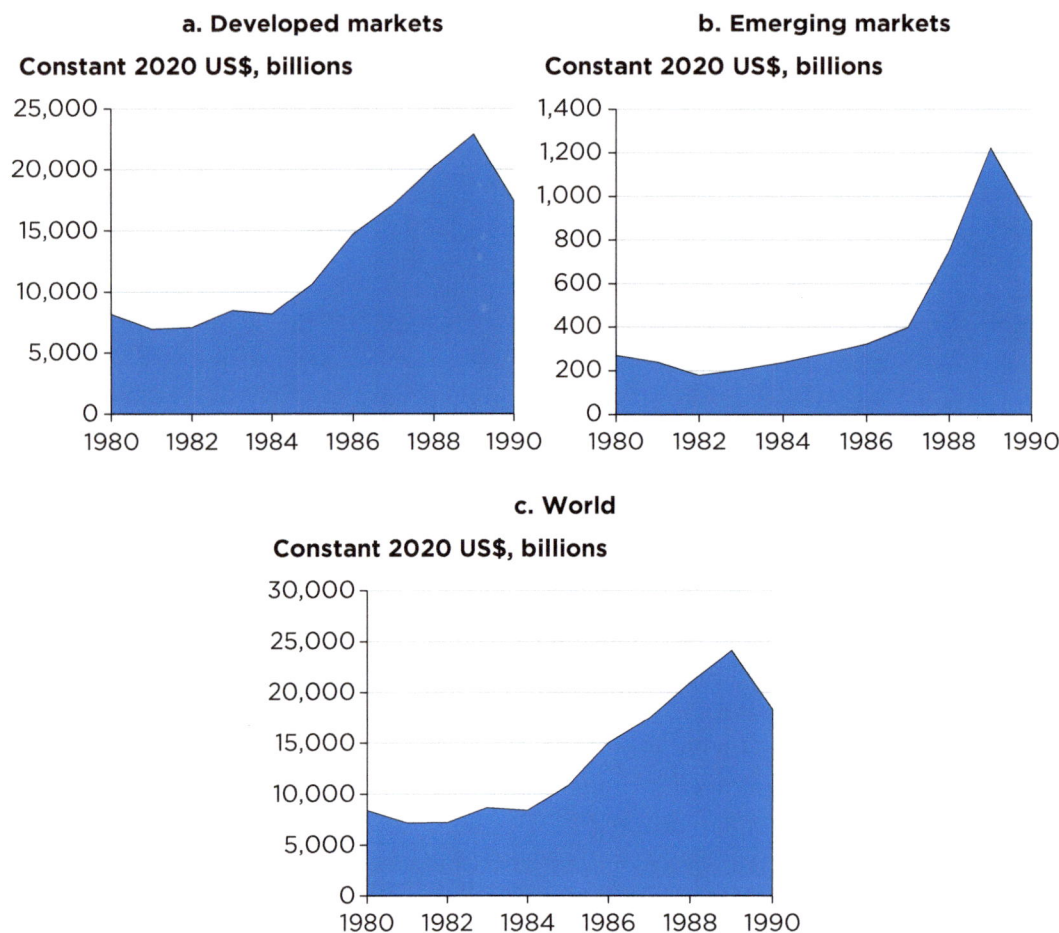

a. Developed markets
Constant 2020 US$, billions

b. Emerging markets
Constant 2020 US$, billions

c. World
Constant 2020 US$, billions

Source: Calculations using market capitalization data and country classifications from the International Finance Corporation's Emerging Stock Markets Factbooks.
Note: This figure presents the global stock market capitalization for 1980–90. The values are in billions of constant 2020 US dollars.

Notes

1. For outstanding corporate bonds, data availability is limited prior to 1990.
2. The developed economies included in the International Finance Corporation's Emerging Stock Markets Factbooks are Australia, Austria, Belgium, Canada, Denmark, France, Germany, Israel, Italy, Japan, the Netherlands, Singapore, Sweden, South Africa, Spain, Switzerland, the United Kingdom, and the United States. The emerging markets included are Argentina; Brazil; Chile; Colombia; Greece; India; Jordan; the Republic of Korea; Malaysia; Mexico; Nigeria; Pakistan; the Philippines; Taiwan, China; Thailand; Türkiye; the República Bolivariana de Venezuela; and Zimbabwe.

APPENDIX F

Global Gross Capital Issuance

An alternative measure of capital market activity is gross capital issuance, the volume of bonds and equity issued each year. As opposed to net issuance, gross issuance for bonds includes maturing bonds that are being rolled over. Examining this indicator can be useful, as firms' ability to roll over bond financing is often critical to their operations, even though it does not register as additional financing.

Annual gross capital issuance surged eightfold from about US$500 billion in 1990 to about US$4 trillion in 2020 (figure F.1). The increasing activity in capital markets is not always obvious when examining cumulative net capital issuance (CNI) because of its aggregated nature over time.

Notably, although cumulative net equity issuance constituted roughly half of the total CNI over 1990–2022, new bonds constituted the majority (72 percent) of gross capital issued each year.

Although gross capital issuance grew steadily throughout 1990–99 and early 2000–09, it was not until the global financial crisis that the growth of capital issuance accelerated significantly. This acceleration was due to the surge in bond issuance that began during the crisis. As the banking system in the United States and other high-income economies was in turmoil, firms worldwide shifted from bank loans to bonds (Adrian, Colla, and Shin 2013; Becker and Ivashina 2014; Cortina, Didier, and Schmukler 2020). The rise in bond issuance abated only in 2020.

FIGURE F.1

Gross Capital Issuance, Primarily New Bonds, Has Grown Globally

Constant 2020 US\$, billions

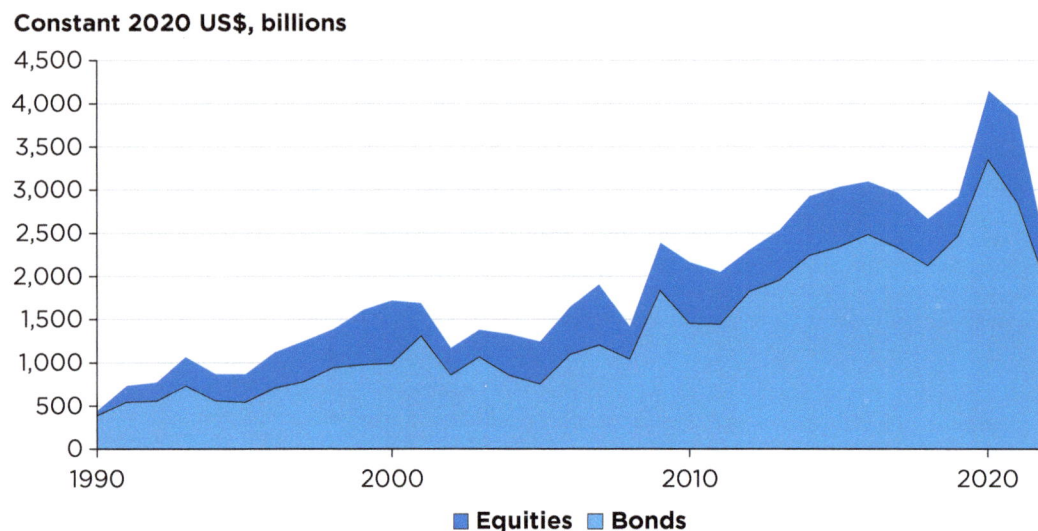

■ Equities ■ Bonds

Source: Calculations using issuance data from the Securities Data Company Platinum database from LSEG.
Note: This figure presents the amount of global gross bond and equity issuance for nonfinancial firms, annually, for 1990–2022 in billions of constant US dollars.

References

Adrian, T., P. Colla, and H. S. Shin. 2013. "Which Financial Frictions? Parsing the Evidence from the Financial Crisis of 2007 to 2009." *NBER Macroeconomics Annual* 27 (1): 159–214.

Becker, B., and V. Ivashina. 2014. "Cyclicality of Credit Supply: Firm Level Evidence." *Journal of Monetary Economics* 62 (March): 76–93.

Cortina, J. J., T. Didier, and S. L. Schmukler. 2020. "Global Corporate Debt during Crises: Implications of Switching Borrowing across Markets." *Journal of International Economics* 131 (July): 103487.

APPENDIX G

Currency of Issuance

While currency of issuance is an important aspect of capital issuance, it is closely linked to the market of issuance, especially for low- and middle-income countries (table G.1): 84 percent of domestic market issuances are in domestic currency, and 93 percent of international issuances are in foreign currency. Since the correlation between market and currency is extremely high, the findings are consistent regardless of whether the market or the currency of issuance is examined.

TABLE G.1

Currency of Issuance Is Closely Tied to the Market of Issuance

Percent of total currency issuance

Market of issuance	Domestic currency	Foreign currency
Domestic market	84.22	15.78
International market	6.68	93.32

Source: Calculations using issuance data from the Securities Data Company Platinum database from LSEG.
Note: This table presents the percentage of domestic and foreign currency issuances by market of issuance in low- and middle-income countries for the 1990–2022 period. Percentages are based on CNI, which is calculated as the sum of equity issuance and bond issuance (minus bonds that matured) since 1990. Appendix B provides the list of countries, grouped by income category. CNI = cumulative net capital issuance.

APPENDIX H

Using 2010 as the Cutoff for New Participants

The purpose of categorizing firms into different participant groups is to assess the entry of new firms into capital markets. To do this, firms are divided into two groups: 1990s participants and new participants. The firms active in capital markets in the 1990s serve as a benchmark against which new participants are compared. Although using the year 2000 as the cutoff between these groups is an arbitrary choice, the results hold regardless of the cutoff year chosen.

Figure H.1 presents charts similar to those in figure 3.3 but uses 2010 as the cutoff year. This means that only firms that first issued capital in or after 2010 during the 1990–2022 period are categorized as new participants.[1] The findings using 2010 as the cutoff year are comparable to those in figure 3.3, which uses 2000 as the cutoff. Specifically, the cumulative net capital issuance (CNI) of new participants has increased over time across all subgroups, and the new participants' share of total CNI in 2022 was higher in low- and middle-income countries and China than in high-income countries.[2]

FIGURE H.1

New Participants Account for a Large Proportion of CNI in Low-
and Middle-Income Countries Regardless of the Cutoff Year Used

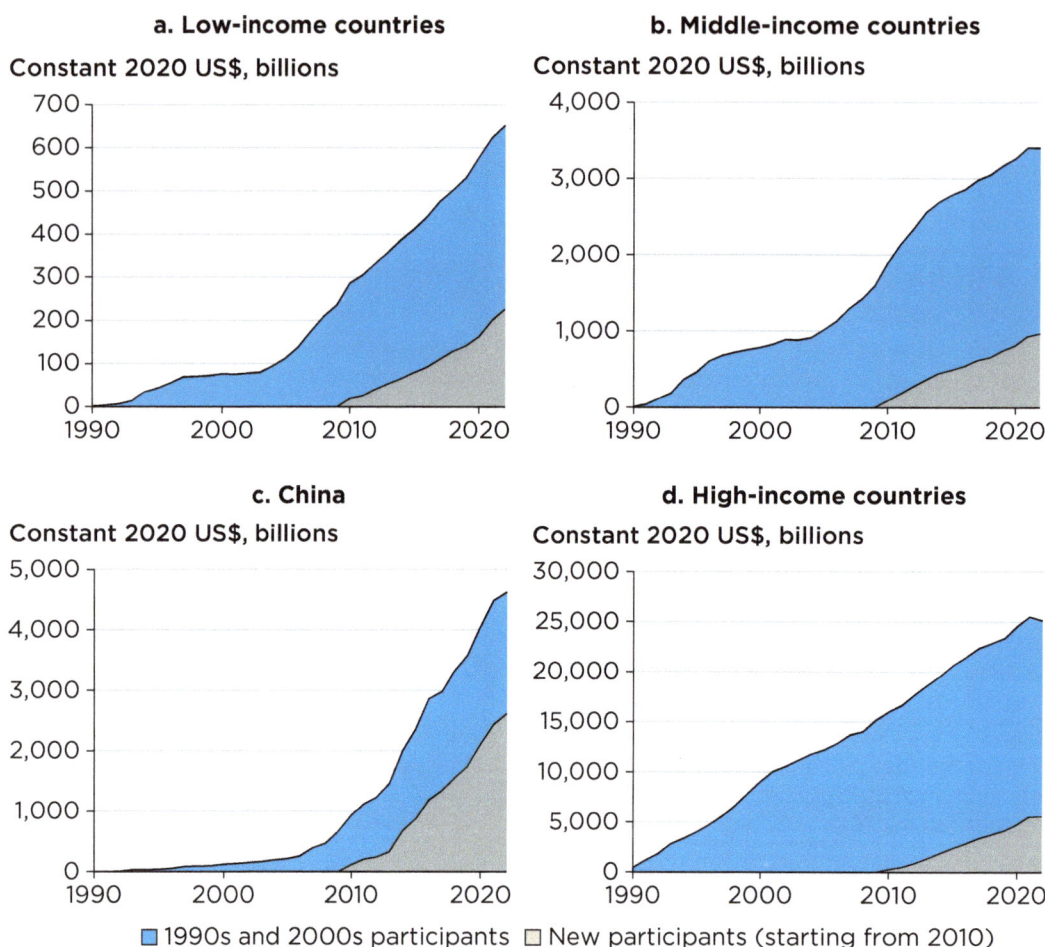

a. Low-income countries

Constant 2020 US$, billions

b. Middle-income countries

Constant 2020 US$, billions

c. China

Constant 2020 US$, billions

d. High-income countries

Constant 2020 US$, billions

■ 1990s and 2000s participants □ New participants (starting from 2010)

Source: Calculations using issuance data from the Securities Data Company Platinum
database from LSEG.
Note: This figure shows the CNI issued by new and 1990s participants for the 1990–2022
period in billions of constant US dollars. CNI for year *Y* is computed as the sum of equity
issuance and bond issuance (minus bonds that matured) between 1990 and year *Y*. Firms
are considered 1990s and 2000s participants if they issued at least once during the
1990s and 2000s and new participants if they issued for the first time from 2010 onward.
Appendix B provides the list of countries, grouped by income category. CNI = cumulative
net capital issuance.

Notes

1. Firms that first issued capital in the 2000s during the 1990–2022 period are no longer categorized as new participants in figure H.1.

2. In 2022, the share of new participant CNI was 22 percent in high-income countries, 28 percent in middle-income countries, 34 percent in low-income countries, and 56 percent in China.

APPENDIX I

Market Share of New Participants across Sectors

New participants have a significantly larger share of cumulative net capital issuance (CNI) across all economic sectors in low- and middle-income countries than in high-income countries (figure I.1). Although new participants raised some capital in 2000–09, most of the growth in issuance occurred in 2010–22. New participants accounted for 50 percent or more of CNI across all sectors in low- and middle-income countries in 2010–22. Conversely, new participants lagged 1990s participants in high-income countries, accounting for less than 50 percent across all sectors.

FIGURE I.1

New Participants' Share of CNI Increased across All Economic Sectors

a. Low- and middle-income countries

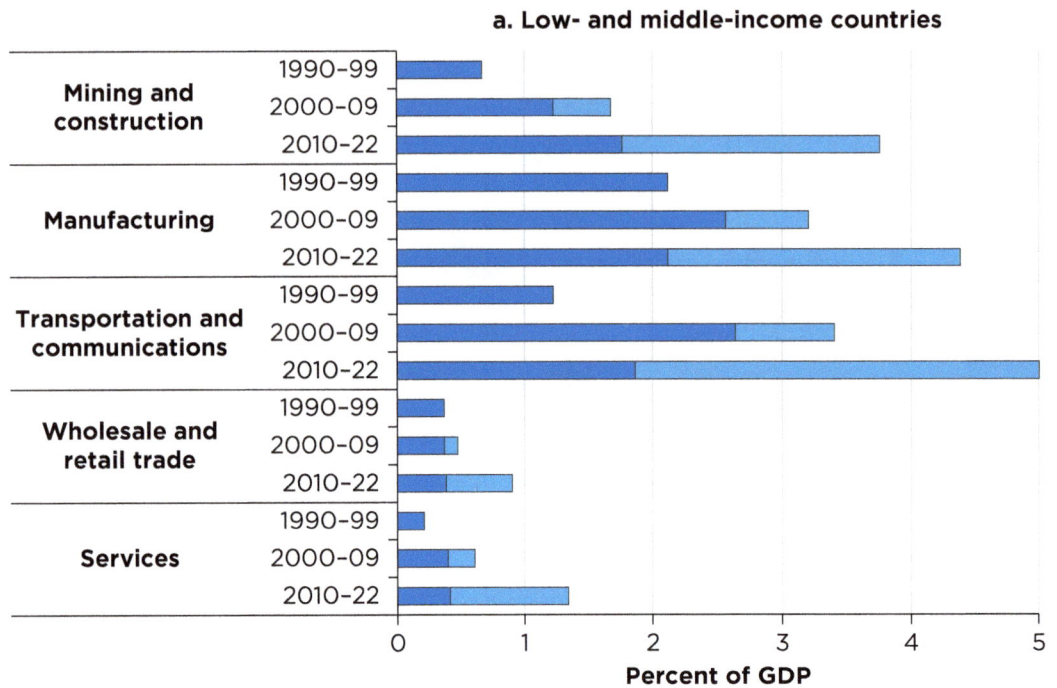

Percent of GDP

continued

FIGURE I.1 *(Continued)*

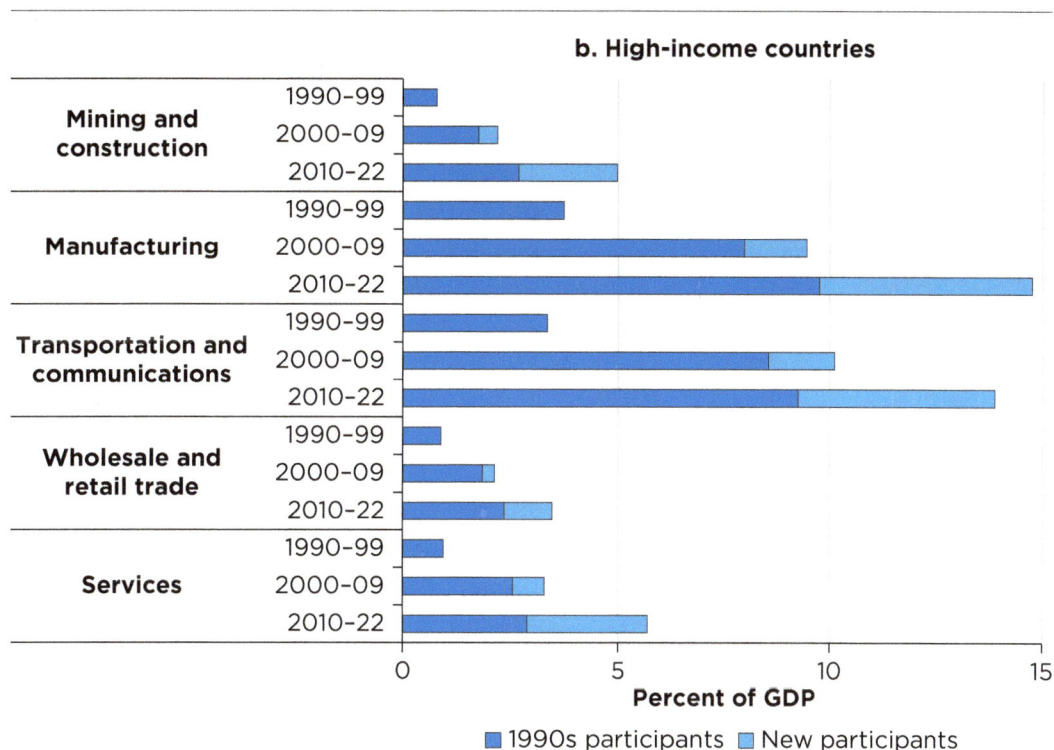

b. High-income countries

Legend: ■ 1990s participants ■ New participants

Source: Calculations using issuance data from the Securities Data Company Platinum database from LSEG and GDP data from the World Bank's World Development Indicators.

Note: This figure shows CNI (as a percentage of GDP) for new participants and 1990s participants in various sectors. CNI as a ratio to GDP for year Y is computed as the sum of equity issuance and bond issuance (minus bonds that matured) between 1990 and year Y, divided by GDP in year Y. The figure reports decade averages for such ratios. Firms are considered 1990s participants if they issued at least once during the 1990s and new participants if they issued for the first time from 2000 onward. Appendix B provides the list of countries, grouped by income category. CNI = cumulative net capital issuance; GDP = gross domestic product.

APPENDIX J

Domestic Market Share in Low- and Middle-Income Countries

The domestic share of cumulative net capital issuance (CNI) has increased over time across all subgroups of low- and middle-income countries (figure J.1). In low-income countries, the domestic market share for new participants' CNI reached 82 percent in 2010–22, up from 75 percent in 2000–09, while for 1990s participants, the domestic share increased to 73 percent, up from 68 percent in 1990–99. Similarly, in middle-income countries, the domestic market share for 1990s participants grew to 70 percent in 2010–22, up from 62 percent in 1990–99, while the share for new participants hovered around 70 percent in 2000–09 and 2010–22. In China, both types of firms have consistently maintained a domestic share above 80 percent across all decades, with the share increasing to more than 90 percent over time. Domestic markets play a critical role in facilitating access to capital markets for all firms in low- and middle-income countries. Meanwhile, new participants in high-income countries are increasingly accessing international markets, perhaps because they are not as constrained to issuing securities in foreign currency when issuing in these markets.

FIGURE J.1

Domestic Market Share Rose in Low- and Middle-Income
Countries and Fell for New Participants in High-Income Countries

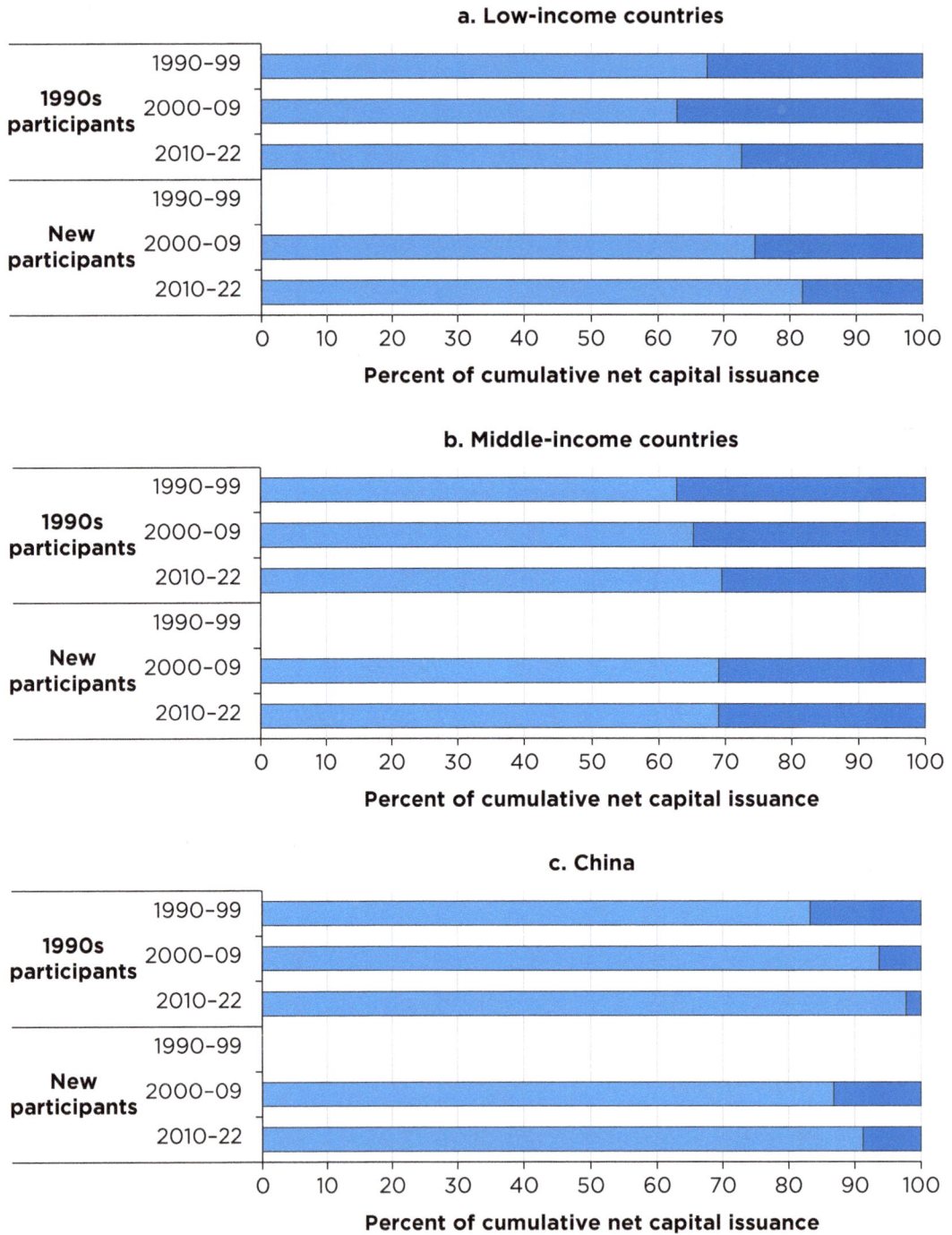

a. Low-income countries

Percent of cumulative net capital issuance

b. Middle-income countries

Percent of cumulative net capital issuance

c. China

Percent of cumulative net capital issuance

continued

FIGURE J.1 *(Continued)*

d. High-income countries

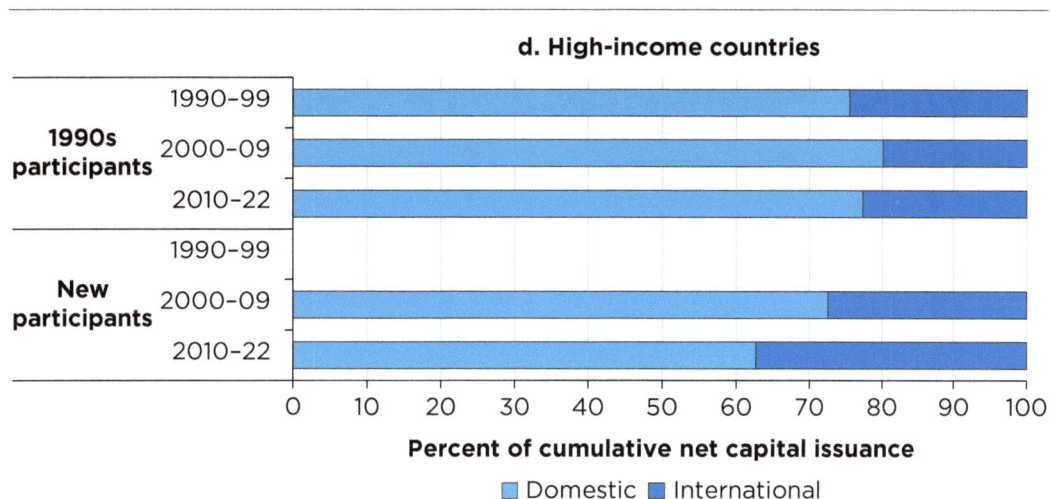

Percent of cumulative net capital issuance

■ Domestic ■ International

Source: Calculations using issuance data from Securities Data Company Platinum database from LSEG.

Note: This figure presents the share of domestic and international market CNI for new and 1990s participants by income group. CNI for year Y is computed as the sum of equity issuance and bond issuance (minus bonds that matured) between 1990 and year Y. The shares are calculated annually and then averaged across decades. Firms are considered 1990s participants if they issued at least once during the 1990s and new participants if they issued for the first time from 2000 onward. Bonds are categorized as domestic or international by comparing the market location of issuance with the residence of the issuing firm. Equity is classified as domestic or international by comparing the location of the primary exchange where a firm's stock trades with the residence of the issuing firm. Appendix B provides the list of countries, grouped by income category. CNI = cumulative net capital issuance.

APPENDIX K

Data Sets of Firms' Issuance Activity and Balance Sheet

The analysis uses two different data sets. First, it uses data on the universe of issuance activity from the Securities Data Company Platinum database from LSEG. Those data yield equity and bond issuances by publicly listed and private firms between 1990 and 2022.[1] Second, it uses publicly listed firms' balance sheets and income statements from the Worldscope database for the same period, 1990–2022.

Worldscope is important because the information on firm balance sheets in the Securities Data Company Platinum database is extremely limited, containing statistics on total assets only. Despite this limitation, focusing on publicly listed firms when analyzing the real effects of the increasing participation of new participants in capital markets is informative. Publicly listed firms account for around 93.2 percent of total assets as measured in the Securities Data Company Platinum database.

A matching procedure is followed to merge the two data sets. The procedure starts by using common identifiers in both databases (such as the LSEG Permanent Identifier, the Committee for Uniform Security Identification Providers identification number, the Stock Exchange Daily Official List, and the International Securities Identification Numbers Organization identifiers) in sequential order. In particular, it starts with the LSEG Permanent Identifier. If the initial matching attempt proves unsuccessful, it uses subsequent identifiers. For companies that remain unmatched through common identifiers, the matching process exploits the company name and country.

The following industries are excluded from the data set: finance, insurance, real estate, and public administration. Also excluded are certain types of issuances (asset-backed, mortgage-backed, and financial credit agency). To maintain comparability across countries and decades, all nominal variables are converted to millions of constant 2011 US dollars.

Most of the analysis is done by aggregating high-income countries and low- and middle-income countries at the country-group level. To do so, two additional variables are used: income classification by the World Bank Group and gross domestic product (GDP) from the World Development Indicators (purchasing power parity series constant 2017 international dollars).[2]

Table K.1 provides several statistics for a set of variables for high-income countries and low- and middle-income countries separately. It reports descriptive statistics at the firm level for issuance activity (in number and value for equity and bonds), age, physical capital, employment, and sales. All the moments—the mean, median, 75th percentile, and 90th percentile—are computed using the pool of firms and years (1990–2022).

The sample consists of 90,133 firms, with 64,768 in high-income countries. Since the focus here is on firms that are active in capital markets and publicly listed, the sample contains large firms. The average amount of sales per year is around US$899 million—US$400 million in low- and middle-income countries and US$1,078 million in high-income countries. The average number of employees is around 3,754 (2,681 in low- and middle-income countries and 4,084 in high-income countries). And the average value of physical capital is US$468 million (US$269 million in low- and middle-income countries and US$539 million in high-income countries).

TABLE K.1

How do the Securities Data Company Platinum and Worldscope Data Sets Describe Firms and Their Activity in Capital Markets?

Characteristic	Low- and middle-income countries					High-income countries				
	Number of firms	Mean	Median	75th percentile	90th percentile	Number of firms	Mean	Median	75th percentile	90th percentile
Sales (US$, millions)	18,312	400	49	172	605	51,144	1,078	63	349	1,612
Employees	13,821	2,681	523	1,648	5,086	44,790	4,084	368	1,697	6,963
Physical capital (US$, millions)	18,263	269	19	78	319	50,784	539	16	113	648
Age	2,978	36	32	48	69	14,613	38	26	56	88
Equity issued per firm (US$, millions)	25,365	76	0	19	103	64,768	199	8	77	339
Bonds issued per firm (US$, millions)	25,365	118	0	3	127	64,768	422	0	0	405
Number of equity issuances per firm	25,365	1	0	1	3	64,768	2	1	3	6
Number of bonds issuances per firm	25,365	2	0	1	4	64,768	2	0	1	3

Source: Calculations using issuance data from the Securities Data Company Platinum database and firm balance characteristics data from Worldscope, both from LSEG.

Note: This table provides several statistics for high-income countries and for low- and middle-income countries separately: descriptive statistics at the firm level for issuance activity (number and value for equity and bonds), age, net property, plant, and equipment (physical capital), number of employees, and net sales. All the moments—the mean, median, 75th percentile, and 90th percentile—are averages computed using the pool of firms and years 1990–2022. Issued value, physical capital, and net sales are all reported in millions of constant 2011 US dollars. Appendix B provides the list of countries, grouped by income category.

These high averages, however, are driven by the right tails of the distributions. For example, 50 percent of the firms in the sample have sales below US$58 million (US$49 million in low-income countries and US$63 million in high-income countries), employment below 404 workers (523 in low- and middle-income countries and 368 in high-income countries), and a level of physical capital below US$17 million (US$19 million in low-income countries and US$16 million in high-income countries). The sample consists of mature firms, with an average and median age of 37 and 27 (36 and 32 in low- and middle-income countries and 38 and 26 in high-income countries).

The average value of equity issued over 1990–2022 per firm is US$164 million (US$76 million in low- and middle-income countries and US$199 million in high-income countries). For bonds, the average value is US$337 million (US$118 million in low- and middle-income countries and US$422 million in high-income countries). However, issuance activities are rare. For example, the average number of equity issuances during the same period was 1.1 in low- and middle-income countries and 2.0 in high-income countries. However, 50 percent of the firms had no issuance in low- and middle-income countries and 1 or fewer equity issuance in high-income countries. For bonds, the average number of issuances was 1.8 in low- and middle-income countries and 1.5 in high-income countries, with 50 percent of the firms exhibiting no bond issuance in either low- and middle-income countries or high-income countries.

Notes

1. Transactions under US$1 million are excluded, and the data are aggregated at the firm-year level.
2. These data sets can be found at the following websites: the World Bank's World Development Indicators Data Bank (https://databank.worldbank.org/reports .aspx?source=2&series=NY.GDP.MKTP.PP.KD&country=) and the World Bank's Country and Lending Groups (https://datahelpdesk.worldbank.org/knowledgebase /articles/906519). The first classification of countries into income groups (gross national income [GNI] per capita in US dollars) was provided in 1987 by the World Bank. However, not all countries were classified until later. For those countries, the first year they appear in the classification is used.

APPENDIX L

Details on the Calculation of Firms' Marginal Return to Capital

A firm's marginal return to capital (MRK), defined as the additional output a firm would produce if an additional unit of capital was allocated to it, is not directly observable. An approach that has become very common in the firm-dynamics literature consists of making assumptions about firms' technology, consumers' preferences, and market structure. Under these assumptions, a researcher can use available firm-level data sets to compute estimates of firms' MRK.

In standard models of firm heterogeneity (for example, Hsieh and Klenow 2009), for firm i in industry s, MRK can be expressed as:

$$MRK_{si} \equiv \alpha_s \left(\frac{\sigma - 1}{\sigma} \right) \left(\frac{P_{si} Y_{si}}{K_{si}} \right), \tag{L.1}$$

where σ refers to the elasticity of substitution across varieties produced by different firms (constant across firms and industries), α_s refers to the output elasticity of capital (constant across firms within the same industry), and $P_{si} Y_{si}$ and K_{si} refer to firms' sales and capital stock, respectively.

Assuming some value for σ and estimating a production function at the industry level to obtain α_s, it is possible to estimate a firm's MRK conditional on observing its sales and stock of capital. Throughout the analysis carried out in the book, a value of $\sigma = 4$ is assumed, a standard value in the literature and between the two values used by Hsieh and Klenow (2009). Details on the production function estimation, needed to estimate α_s at the industry level, follow.

For estimating the production function, assume that firms producing in a given industry have access to a Cobb-Douglas production function of the following form:

$$y_{its} = \alpha_0 + \gamma_s l_{its} + \alpha_s k_{its} + \epsilon_{its}, \qquad (L.2)$$

where y_{its} refers to firm output (in logs), l_{its} refers to firm labor (in logs), k_{its} refers to firm capital (in logs), and ϵ_{its} is an error term. The coefficients of interest are the output elasticities of labor and capital, γ_s and α_s. The main issue when estimating this equation is the existence of a simultaneity problem: part of the error term—for example, a persistent productivity shock—may affect output and capital at the same time, hence biasing the estimates of α_s. Levinsohn and Petrin (2003) propose solving this issue by using an additional flexible input in the estimation—for example, materials—containing information about the underlying productivity shock.

To estimate production functions at the industry level, a version of Levinsohn and Petrin (2003) is implemented by using the Stata command *levpet*. The inputs required in that command are a measure of firms' output (which are proxied by firm value added), a measure of firms' employment (for which the number of employees is used), a measure of firms' capital (for which physical capital is used), and a measure of an additional flexible input (for which raw materials are used). The estimation is performed at the one-digit SIC (Standard Industry Classification) using firms from all countries producing in that industry. The number of observations used in the estimation varies by industry, ranging from 3,567 to 22,000.

Results: α_s and γ_s are estimated very precisely across all industries, with all the estimates being significant at 1 percent. The average estimated value of α_s is 0.30, with a standard deviation of 0.10 and ranging from 0.10 to 0.44. In the case of γ_s, the average estimate is 0.42, with a standard deviation of 0.15 and ranging from 0.24 to 0.70.

References

Hsieh, C.-T., and P. J. Klenow. 2009. "Misallocation and Manufacturing TFP in China and India." *Quarterly Journal of Economics* 124 (4): 1403–48.

Levinsohn, J., and A. Petrin. 2003. "Estimating Production Functions Using Inputs to Control for Unobservables." *Review of Economic Studies* 70 (2): 317–41.

APPENDIX M

Dispersion in the Marginal Returns to Capital across Firms

Understanding why firms exhibit a high or a low marginal return to capital (MRK) has been central in the literature investigating the causes and consequences of misallocating resources across firms in low- and middle-income countries. In theoretical models of heterogeneous firms, several factors can explain the dispersion in MRK across firms within an industry-country. One is the presence of adjustment costs (Asker, Collard-Wexler, and de Loecker 2014). For example, a firm will not adjust its capital stock after receiving a positive demand shock if that shock is temporary—so it will temporarily exhibit a relatively high MRK. Another is related to information frictions—firms may not know their level of demand or productivity when deciding how much capital to install (David, Hopenhayn, and Venkateswaran 2016). A firm that receives an unexpectedly high demand shock will also exhibit a relatively high MRK. A third factor is heterogeneity in firm-level risk (David, Schmid, and Zeke 2022). A firm whose risk is perceived as high will have to pay a risk premium in its interest rate, reducing the firm's demand for capital and thus exhibiting a high MRK.

Perhaps the most common interpretation of dispersion in firm MRK is that different firms may have differential access to credit (Gopinath et al. 2017). If a firm exhibits a relatively high MRK, the potential gain from using additional capital is high. The fact that the firm remains with a high MRK reflects its inability to obtain capital, indicating that it is financially constrained. Otherwise, the firm would expand to exploit business opportunities.

References

Asker, J., A. Collard-Wexler, and J. de Loecker. 2014. "Dynamic Inputs and Resource (Mis)Allocation." *Journal of Political Economy* 122 (5): 1013–63.

David, J. M., H. A. Hopenhayn, and V. Venkateswaran. 2016. "Information, Misallocation, and Aggregate Productivity." *Quarterly Journal of Economics* 131 (2): 943–1005.

David, J. M., L. Schmid, and D. Zeke. 2022. "Risk-Adjusted Capital Allocation and Misallocation." *Journal of Financial Economics* 145 (3): 684–705.

Gopinath, G., Ş. Kalemli-Özcan, L. Karabarbounis, and C. Villegas-Sanchez. 2017. "Capital Allocation and Productivity in South Europe." *Quarterly Journal of Economics* 132 (4): 1915–67. https://doi.org/10.1093/qje/qjx024.

APPENDIX N

Calculations of the Aggregate Effects

At a given point in time, the change in aggregate capital (labor) in a particular industry and country can be computed as the sum of the changes in capital (labor) across all firms operating in that industry-country, weighted by each firm's relative size. In the case of capital, for example, at a given point in time, the evolution of aggregate capital in a given industry s and country c is given by:

$$\frac{K_{t+1}}{K_t} = \sum_i \omega_{i,t} \frac{K_{i,t+1}}{K_{i,t}},\tag{N.1}$$

where the first term in the right-hand side is firm i's share of physical capital in its industry-country at time t, and the second term is the change in capital of firm i. Intuitively, this expression implies that the change in aggregate capital depends on how much firms change their capital interacted with their relative size in the industry-country where they operate.

This accounting identity can be used to estimate the strength of the association between firms' issuance activity and the evolution of aggregate capital and labor. With that goal in mind, the following regression is run:

$$\%\Delta k_{i,t+1} \equiv \frac{k_{i,t+1} - k_{i,t}}{k_{i,t}} = \alpha_i + \alpha_{s(i)t} + \alpha_{c(i)t} + \beta_1 x_{it} + \beta_2 x_{it} * \mathbb{1}\{i = NP\} + \varepsilon_{it},\tag{N.2}$$

where the α_s refer to firm fixed effects, industry-year fixed effects, and country-year fixed effects. The variable x_{it} measures firms' activity in capital markets (measured in log value of issuances). These regressions are similar to the local projections run in chapter 4, with a few minor differences that make them consistent with the aggregate accounting identity. For example, issuance activity on the right-hand side of this regression is measured as the log value issued by the firm, as opposed to a dummy simply capturing whether the firm exhibited an issuance episode in that year. These regressions deliver the same qualitative results as the ones shown above: firms' issuance activity is associated with an increase in their capital and labor, with this relationship being stronger for new participants.

Issuance activity is followed by an increase in both capital and employment, particularly for new participants. In the case of physical capital, for example, the estimated coefficients imply that issuances in capital markets of a value similar to the median issuance (US$46 million) are associated with an extra increase in physical capital of around 2.0 percentage points for active participants in the 1990s and around 2.5 percentage points for new participants. For the average issuance value (US$250 million), the estimated effect would imply an extra increase in physical capital of around 3.0 percentage points for 1990s participants and 3.6 percentage points for new participants.

Given these estimates, the change in physical capital predicted by issuance activity for each firm-year is given by the following expression (a similar expression applies for the case of employment):

$$\widehat{\%\Delta k_{i,t+1}} = \hat{\beta}_1 x_{it} + \hat{\beta}_2 x_{it} * \mathbb{1}\{i = \text{NP}\}. \tag{N.3}$$

This expression is interpreted as the change in physical capital of a given firm i in a given year t predicted by its capital market activity. Aggregating this equation across all firms in the sample using the accounting identity described above yields the change in aggregate capital in a given industry-country-year predicted by capital markets. Computing a weighted average of these predicted changes across industries yields the change in physical capital predicted by capital market activities at the country level. Figure 4.6 reports the difference between these predicted cumulative changes between 2000 and 2022 (under the observed capital market activity) and an alternative scenario with no capital market activity.

Chapter 4 also analyzes the association between firms' capital market activity and aggregate productivity. Following the previous literature (for example, Baqaee and Farhi 2019; Bau and Matray 2023; Petrin and Levinsohn 2012), this analysis uses a first-order approximation of the change in productivity in a given industry-country at a given point in time:[1]

$$\Delta \text{Productivity}_t \approx \sum_i \omega_{i,t} \; \alpha^k \; \frac{\tau_{it}}{1 + \tau_{it}} \Delta \ln k_{i,t}, \tag{N.4}$$

where $\tau_{it} \equiv MRK_{it} / r - 1$.

Productivity refers to the "Solow residual" in a given industry-country. That is, it measures a residual factor influencing output once factors of production have been accounted for; $\omega_{i,t}$ refers to the share of sales of firm i of all sales in its country-industry; α^k is the output elasticity with respect to input capital; and r refers to the rental rate of capital. Following Hsieh and Klenow (2009), a value of $r = 10$ percent is assumed.

Equation N.4 shows how the allocation of capital to firms with different levels of MRK can affect productivity in the economy. In an economy without distortions—that is, all firms have an MRK equal to the same rental rate—changes in the total amount and distribution of capital have no effect on productivity. In an economy with distortions, productivity increases if capital is allocated relatively more to firms that are financially constrained—that is, firms whose marginal product is higher than the cost of capital. On the contrary, productivity in the economy decreases if capital is allocated relatively more to firms that are "subsidized"—that is, firms whose marginal product is lower than the cost of capital.

To study the association between firms' activity in capital markets and productivity, the change in physical capital at the firm level predicted by issuance activity is plugged into the productivity equation (equation N.4). Applying the productivity equation to firms in the sample yields the change in productivity in a given industry-country-year that is predicted by capital markets. Computing a weighted average of these predicted changes across industries yields the change in productivity that is predicted by capital market activities at the country level. As in the case of physical capital, figure 4.6 reports the difference between these predicted cumulative changes between 2000 and 2022 (under the observed capital market activity) and an alternative scenario with no capital market activity.

Note

1. The full expression also includes a within-firm component and the same allocation component for other factors of production. The analysis here focuses on the effects on productivity resulting from the allocation of capital.

References

Baqaee, D. R., and E. Farhi. 2019. "A Short Note on Aggregating Productivity." NBER Working Paper 25688, National Bureau of Economic Research, Cambridge, MA.

Bau, N., and A. Matray. 2023. "Misallocation and Capital Market Integration: Evidence from India." *Econometrica* 91 (1): 67–106.

Hsieh, C.-T., and P. J. Klenow. 2009. "Misallocation and Manufacturing TFP in China and India." *Quarterly Journal of Economics* 124 (4): 1403–48.

Petrin, A., and J. Levinsohn. 2012. "Measuring Aggregate Productivity Growth Using Plant-Level Data." *RAND Journal of Economics* 43 (4): 705–25.

APPENDIX O

Methodology for Event Studies

The methodology for the event studies analyzing pension reforms (figure 5.2 in chapter 5) and liberalization episodes (figure 5.3) is a staggered difference-in-differences (DiD) approach, as in Freyaldenhoven, Hansen, and Shapiro (2019). The approach is designed to evaluate the effects of these policy changes on capital markets in low- and middle-income countries. This approach captures dynamic treatment effects over time, accommodating variations in the timing of reforms across countries.

What Is the Baseline Model?

The baseline model is represented by the following equation:

$$Y_{it} = \alpha_i + \lambda_t + \sum_{k \neq -1} \beta_k D_{i,t+k} + \varepsilon_{it}, \qquad (O.1)$$

where

- Y_{it} is the outcome variable, representing the ratio of cumulative net issuances to gross domestic product (GDP) for country i in year t;

- α_i and λ_t are country and year fixed effects, respectively, controlling for time-invariant country characteristics and common shocks across years; and

- ε_{it} is the error term.

The term $D_{i,t+k}$ is an indicator variable that equals 1 if country i is in period k relative to its treatment year, where $k = 0$ is the year of treatment (that is, the year of pension reform in the first event study or liberalization episode in the second event study). The model considers event time windows, with $k > 0$ representing posttreatment periods and $k < 0$ representing pretreatment periods. The period $k = -1$ serves as the baseline period and acts as a reference point for estimating treatment effects. The coefficients β_k capture the dynamic treatment effect at each event time k, illustrating how the outcome evolves relative to the baseline period. The coefficients β_k and associated confidence intervals are plotted in figures 5.2 and 5.3 for the pension reforms and liberalization episodes, respectively.

Control countries, which never receive treatment, have all D indicators set to zero. These control units are essential for identifying the common time effects λ_t and defining a counterfactual trend for treated countries. This methodology relies on the parallel trend assumption, where untreated countries serve as a benchmark for estimating the counterfactual outcomes in treated countries in the absence of reform. To account for macroeconomic factors, GDP growth is included as a control variable, reflecting the role of economic growth in shaping capital markets, as discussed in chapter 5.

Placebo Tests Validate the Results

Pension Reforms

To validate the results, a placebo pension reform year was randomly assigned between 1993 and 2020 to control countries that never implemented an actual reform. The staggered DiD model was reestimated using this placebo data to test for any before and after differences in cumulative net capital issuances. If the original results were due to noise, similar effects would be observed in this placebo test. While the placebo results are precisely estimated due to the large sample of 117 control countries, the economic effects are negligible, showing changes of only 0.2 percent to 0.5 percent in domestic issuances relative to the baseline year ($t - 1$). When compared to the substantial increase in domestic issuances in countries with actual reforms, these values are considered economically insignificant, as illustrated in figure O.1.

FIGURE O.1

The Placebo Test Validates the Findings for Pension Reform

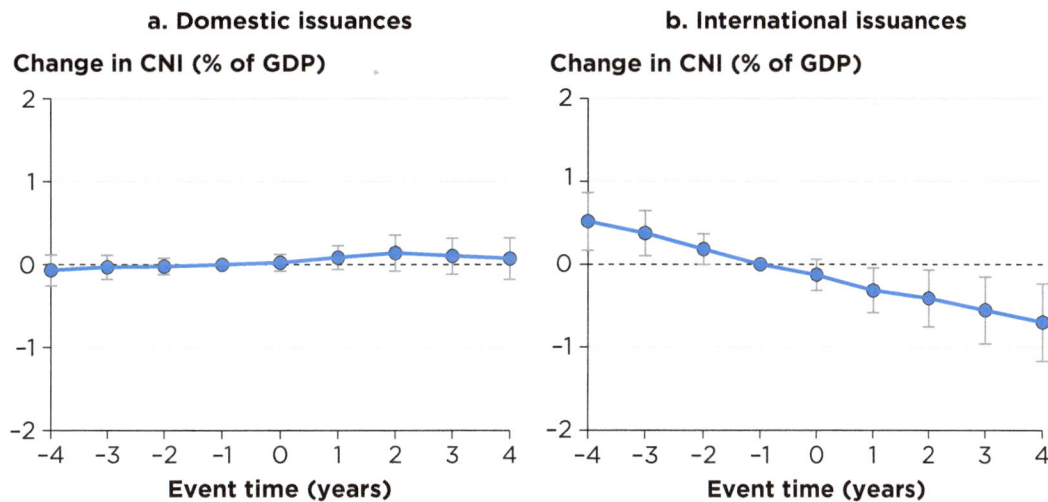

a. Domestic issuances

b. International issuances

Source: Calculations using data from the Securities Data Company Platinum database from LSEG and the International Federation of Pension Fund Administrators and GDP data from the World Bank's World Development Indicators.

Note: The figure shows the results from a placebo test on the impact of pension reforms on domestic (panel a) and foreign (panel b) issuance activity. The placebo exercise assigns a pension reform event randomly across years to a control group consisting of 117 countries that did not implement any major pension reform between 1993 and 2020. The event year is defined as the year of the placebo major pension reform in each country. The vertical axis shows the total change in CNI as a proportion of GDP relative to the year before the reform. CNI for year Y is computed as the sum of equity issuance and bond issuance (minus bonds that matured) between 1990 and year Y. In the baseline year ($t = -1$), domestic and foreign CNI were 5.7 percent and 5.5 percent of GDP, respectively. Point estimates are presented with 95 percent confidence intervals, controlling for year and country fixed effects. CNI = cumulative net capital issuance; GDP = gross domestic product.

Liberalization Policies

Similarly, placebo liberalization episodes were randomly assigned to control countries between 2000 and 2020, and the staggered DiD model was applied to this placebo data. The results reveal no significant effects following the assigned liberalization episodes, with no observable changes in capital market activity (figure O.2). Therefore, the observed increase in international debt issuance after actual liberalization events is not attributable to random variation but specifically reflects the impact of the liberalization policies.

FIGURE O.2

The Placebo Test Validates the Findings for Liberalization
Episodes

a. Domestic debt

Change in CNI (% of GDP)

b. International debt

Change in CNI (% of GDP)

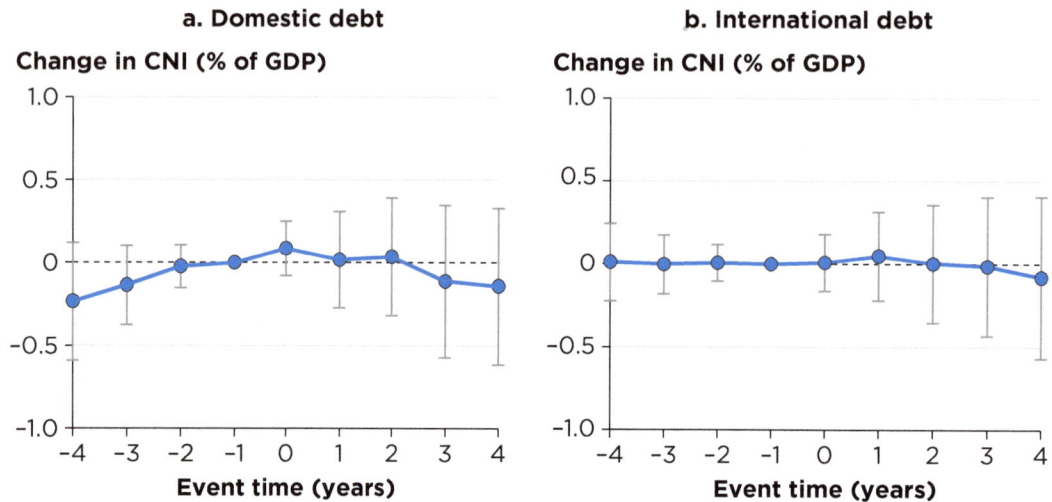

Source: Calculations using data from the Securities Data Company Platinum database
from LSEG and Chinn-Ito databases and GDP data from the World Bank's World
Development Indicators.

Note: The figure shows the results from a placebo test on the impact of liberalization
episodes on domestic (panel a) and foreign (panel b) issuance activity. The placebo
exercise assigns a liberalization event randomly across years to a control group
consisting of 132 countries that did not experience any major liberalization episode
between 2000 and 2020. The event year is defined as the year of the placebo
liberalization episode in each country. The vertical axis shows the total change in CNI as
a proportion of GDP relative to the year before the liberalization episode. Debt CNI for
year Y is computed as the sum of bond issuance (minus bonds that matured) between
1990 and year Y. Point estimates are presented with 95 percent confidence intervals,
controlling for year and country fixed effects. CNI = cumulative net capital issuance;
GDP gross domestic product.

Reference

Freyaldenhoven, S., C. Hansen, and J. M. Shapiro. 2019. "Pre-event Trends in the Panel
    Event-Study Design." *American Economic Review* 109 (9): 3307–38.

APPENDIX P

How Firms Can Improve Their Access to Capital Market Financing

Barriers to participating in capital markets are high for firms in low- and middle-income countries due to the elevated risks associated with investing in them. High risks not only make issuances by firms less attractive to investors but also increase the transaction costs charged by financial intermediaries in the issuance process (such as underwriters and credit rating agencies). These issues disproportionately affect small, young firms, characteristics typical of new participants, inhibiting their entry into capital markets. Such firms face higher informational barriers, as information-gathering costs are higher for less visible firms with limited publicly available information on their operations and performance (Pagano, Panetta, and Zingales 1998). They also face higher transaction costs (Calomiris 2010; Zervos 2004). Transaction costs tend to be partly fixed, creating additional hurdles for small, young firms, given their limited financial capacity (BIS 2019; OECD 2015b; WFE 2018).

Firms can mitigate such information and cost barriers. By improving information flows, firms can reduce the risk not only for investors, hence lowering the cost of capital, but also for intermediaries involved in the issuance process, also lowering transaction costs. Other private sector participants—underwriters, credit rating agencies, and research firms—can also play a part.

Strengthen Shareholder and Bondholder Rights

Strong shareholder rights offer possible remedy for the potential misuse of funds by firm management; they can be especially valuable in the face of high information asymmetries and thus potentially lower the cost of capital for firms (Houston, Lin, and Xie 2018). Of particular relevance is the treatment of minority shareholders by controlling shareholders, a prominent corporate governance issue for investors in low- and middle-income countries (IFC 2018). Shareholder rights also influence transaction costs, with underwriter spreads on equity issuances higher, on average, when such rights are particularly weak (Autore et al. 2018).

Stronger bond covenants protect bondholders by restricting issuers from certain actions that increase the risk to them after issuance. They may include, but are not limited to, restricting additional debt, large dividend payouts, and divestment of major assets by issuers. Bondholders are more likely to seek such protections when an issuer's risk profile is high (OECD 2022), making them particularly relevant for new participants because they are smaller, younger, and more financially constrained than 1990s participants. Evidence of a trade-off between expected returns and bondholder protection suggests that firms could lower financing costs by including such covenants (OECD 2015a).

Improve Firm Corporate Governance and Disclosure

Corporate governance mechanisms reduce agency conflicts between various stakeholders in firms (especially managers and investors). Improving corporate governance reduces potential misuse of corporate resources, including investor capital, and is therefore important for investors. For example, firms with more independent corporate boards (with stronger outside control) and greater institutional investor ownership have better access to capital market financing (Bhojraj and Sengupta 2003; Skaife, Collins, and LaFond 2004).

Investors are also sensitive to managerial entrenchment (supermajority requirements or staggered boards) and earnings manipulation (misreporting information) (Ghouma 2017). The effect of corporate governance on firm's access to capital market financing is more pronounced in markets with weak investor protections (Chen, Chen, and Wei 2009; Durnev and Kim 2005). This effect is particularly true for firms with good investment opportunities, including new participants, which exhibit high marginal returns to capital. Better corporate governance is also documented to reduce the transaction costs of issuing equity (Chen, Goyal, and Zolotoy 2022). Nevertheless, corporate governance is lower, on average, in markets with weak legal systems (Klapper and Love 2004), underscoring the need for firms in low- and middle-income countries to make such improvements. In particular, state- and family-owned firms in low- and middle-income countries tend to exhibit poor corporate governance and could benefit the most from undertaking such measures (Lima and Sanvicente 2013).

Relatedly, the level and quality of disclosure by firms are also linked to capital market financing (Sengupta 1998). Better disclosure can reduce the cost of acquiring information for investors and other third parties engaged in the issuance process (underwriters and credit rating agencies), allowing them to assess firm quality more accurately. Furthermore, it can discourage agency conflicts (Armstrong, Guay, and Weber 2010) and thus complement other corporate governance measures.

Engage with Third-Party Information Providers

Analyst coverage and credit ratings can signal firm quality to investors. Greater analyst coverage increases firms' levels of equity financing, especially for the smallest firms (Derrien and Kecskés 2013). Not only the quantity but also the quality of analyst coverage matters; firms followed by analysts hired by the lead underwriter or with a high-quality reputation also benefit from a lower likelihood of underpricing in equity issuances (Bowen, Chen, and Cheng 2008). Credit ratings can also reduce information asymmetry in both primary equity and bond markets (McBrayer 2019). Firms that obtain a credit rating are nine times more likely to issue a first-time bond than those that do not (Pattani, Vera, and Wackett 2011). The presence of an issuer rating (irrespective of the rating value) may reduce initial public offering (IPO) underpricing, in effect lowering the cost of capital (An and Chan 2008). In subsequent issuances, firms with issuer credit ratings pay lower investment banking fees (McBrayer 2019).

Seek an Anchor Investor for IPOs

Firms should seek to engage an anchor investor, which is typically an institutional investor that buys a significant number of shares being issued, in the IPO premarket (prior to public filing), where regulation allows. An anchor investor reduces underwriter risk (by lowering the likelihood of undersubscription) and sends a credible signal to other investors. Anchor-backed IPOs have lower issuance costs than their non-anchor-backed counterparts (Seth, Vishwanatha, and Prasad 2019). Research on Indian firms shows that engaging anchor investors lowers issuance costs and significantly increases the volume of IPOs (Sharma, Singhal, and Ramanna 2024).[1] And firms that engage anchor investors are more likely to increase capital investments. These effects are stronger for high-growth and financially constrained firms, so new participants may benefit more from seeking an anchor investor. Anchor investors are especially important in hard-to-place offerings, which can include those in less developed markets.

Note

1. The Securities and Exchange Board of India passed regulations in 2009 allowing firms to allocate shares on a preferential basis to anchor investors prior to public filing, with the requirement that firms disclose the share price and the identity of the anchor investors.

References

An, H., and K. C. Chan. 2008. "Credit Ratings and IPO Pricing." *Journal of Corporate Finance* 14 (5): 584–95.

Armstrong, C. S., W. R. Guay, and J. P. Weber. 2010. "The Role of Information and Financial Reporting in Corporate Governance and Debt Contracting." *Journal of Accounting and Economics* 50 (2-3): 179–234.

Autore, D. M., J. Hobbs, T. Kovacs, and V. Singh. 2018. "Do Shareholder Rights Influence the Direct Costs of Issuing Seasoned Equity?" *Review of Quantitative Finance and Accounting* 52 (1): 1–33. https://doi.org/10.1007/s11156-018-0701-1.

Bhojraj, S., and P. Sengupta. 2003. "Effect of Corporate Governance on Bond Ratings and Yields: The Role of Institutional Investors and Outside Directors." *Journal of Business* 76 (3): 455–75. https://doi.org/10.1086/344114.

BIS (Bank for International Settlements). 2019. "Establishing Viable Capital Markets." CGFS Paper 62, Bank for International Settlements, Basel, Switzerland.

Bowen, R. M., X. Chen, and Q. Cheng. 2008. "Analyst Coverage and the Cost of Raising Equity Capital: Evidence from Underpricing of Seasoned Equity Offerings." *Contemporary Accounting Research* 25 (3): 657–700. https://doi.org/10.1506/car.25.3.1.

Calomiris, C. W. 2010. "Underwriting Costs of Seasoned Equity Offerings: Cross-Sectional Determinants and Technological Change, 1980–2008." Working Paper, Columbia Business School, New York.

Chen, K. C. W., Z. Chen, and K. C. J. Wei. 2009. "Legal Protection of Investors, Corporate Governance, and the Cost of Equity Capital." *Journal of Corporate Finance* 15 (3): 273–89. https://doi.org/10.1016/j.jcorpfin.2009.01.001.

Chen, Y., A. Goyal, and L. Zolotoy. 2022. "Global Board Reforms and the Pricing of IPOs." *Journal of Financial and Quantitative Analysis* 57 (6): 2412–43.

Derrien, F., and A. Kecskés. 2013. "The Real Effects of Financial Shocks: Evidence from Exogenous Changes in Analyst Coverage." *Journal of Finance* 68 (4): 1407–40. https://doi.org/10.1111/jofi.12042.

Durnev, A., and E. H. Kim. 2005. "To Steal or Not to Steal: Firm Attributes, Legal Environment, and Valuation." *Journal of Finance* 60 (3): 1461–93.

Ghouma, H. 2017. "How Does Managerial Opportunism Affect the Cost of Debt Financing?" *Research in International Business and Finance* 39 (pt. A, January): 13–29.

Houston, J. F., C. Lin, and W. Xie. 2018. "Shareholder Protection and the Cost of Capital." *Journal of Law and Economics* 61 (4): 677–710. https://doi.org/10.1086/700269.

IFC (International Finance Corporation). 2018. *Corporate Governance Progression Matrix for Listed Companies*. Washington, DC: World Bank.

Klapper, L. F., and I. Love. 2004. "Corporate Governance, Investor Protection, and Performance in Emerging Markets." *Journal of Corporate Finance* 10 (5): 703–28. https://doi.org/10.1016/s0929-1199(03)00046-4.

Lima, B. F., and A. Z. Sanvicente. 2013. "Quality of Corporate Governance and Cost of Equity in Brazil." *Journal of Applied Corporate Finance* 25 (1): 72–80.

McBrayer, G. 2019. "Credit Ratings and the Cost of Issuing Seasoned Equity." *Journal of Financial Research* 42 (2): 303–30. https://doi.org/10.1111/jfir.12171.

OECD (Organisation for Economic Co-operation and Development). 2015a. "Corporate Bonds, Bondholders, and Corporate Governance." OECD Corporate Governance Working Paper, OECD Publishing, Paris. https://doi.org/10.1787/5js69lj4hvnw-en.

OECD (Organisation for Economic Co-operation and Development). 2015b. *Growth Companies, Access to Capital Markets, and Corporate Governance*. Paris: OECD Publishing.

OECD (Organisation for Economic Co-operation and Development). 2022. *The Role and Rights of Debtholders in Corporate Governance*. Paris: OECD Publishing.

Pagano, M., F. Panetta, and L. Zingales. 1998. "Why Do Companies Go Public? An Empirical Analysis." *Journal of Finance* 53 (1): 27–64. https://doi.org/10.1111/0022-1082.25448.

Pattani, A., G. Vera, and J. Wackett. 2011. "Going Public: UK Companies' Use of Capital Markets." *Bank of England Quarterly Bulletin* 51 (4): 319–30.

Sengupta, P. 1998. "Corporate Disclosure Quality and the Cost of Debt." *Accounting Review* 73 (4): 459–74. https://www.jstor.org/stable/248186.

Seth, R., S. R. Vishwanatha, and D. Prasad. 2019. "Allocation to Anchor Investors, Underpricing, and the After-market Performance of IPOs." *Financial Management* 48 (1): 159–86.

Sharma, A., A. Singhal, and V. S. Ramanna. 2024. "The Effect of Lead Institutional Investors on Investment and Capital Structure of Young Firms: Evidence from Indian IPOs." *International Review of Financial Analysis* 91 (January): 102996.

Skaife, H. A., D. W. Collins, and R. LaFond. 2004. "Corporate Governance and the Cost of Equity Capital." *SSRN Electronic Journal*. https://doi.org/10.2139/ssrn.639681.

WFE (World Federation of Exchanges). 2018. "SME Financing and Equity Markets." World Federation of Exchanges, London.

Zervos, S. 2004. "The Transactions Costs of Primary Market Issuance: The Case of Brazil, Chile, and Mexico." Policy Research Working Paper, World Bank, Washington, DC. https://doi.org/10.1596/1813-9450-3424.

ABBREVIATIONS

BIS — Bank for International Settlements
CGFS — Committee on the Global Financial System
CNI — cumulative net capital issuance
DiD — difference-in-differences
GDP — gross domestic product
GFDD — Global Financial Development Database
GNI — gross national income
HHI — Herfindahl-Hirschman Index
IPO — initial public offering
LSEG — London Stock Exchange Group
MRK — marginal return to capital
P25 — 25th percentile
P50 — 50th percentile
P75 — 75th percentile
P90 — 90th percentile
R&D — research and development
SAR — special administrative region
SDC — Securities Data Company Platinum
SDR — Special Drawing Rights
SIC — Standard Industrial Classification
SOE — state-owned enterprise
Std. dev. — standard deviation

www.ingramcontent.com/pod-product-compliance
Lightning Source LLC
Chambersburg PA
CBHW050907210326
41597CB00002B/53